Rural Wales

RURAL WALES

Community and Marginalization

Paul Cloke   Mark Goodwin   Paul Milbourne

UNIVERSITY OF WALES PRESS • CARDIFF • 1997

British Library Cataloguing-in-Publication Data.
A catalogue record for this book is available from
the British Library.

ISBN 0-7083-1365-5

Typeset at Action Typesetting, Gloucester
Printed in Great Britain by Dinefwr Press, Llandybïe

Contents

Acknowledgements

We would like to acknowledge the support of all those who have helped at various stages in the production of this book. We owe thanks to them all. The Welsh Office, the Welsh Development Agency and the Development Board for Rural Wales provided funding for the original research. Graham Joyce, Stephen Bibby, Gwenan Party, Owen Hooker and Vic McPhearson from these agencies served on a steering group which met regularly with the authors throughout the research. The research questionnaire itself was administered by a team of twenty-three staff, and colleagues on the Lifestyles in Rural England project helped to discuss ideas and issues. Simon Godden, at the University of Bristol, and Anthony Smith and Ian Gully, at the University of Wales, Aberystwyth, responded to urgent requests for new diagrams with their usual professionalism. Extracts from the poem 'A Peasant' are reproduced on page 146 by kind permission of the poet R. S. Thomas. Ned Thomas, Ceinwen Jones and Liz Powell from the University of Wales Press supervised the commissioning and production of the book itself. We are grateful to all these for the help that they have given. Perhaps our greatest debt of gratitude, however, is to the people of rural Wales who gave so freely of their time in order to help with our research. Their patience and courtesy in answering our enquiries provided the raw material on which this book is built. Without them the book would not have been possible. We hope that we have conveyed their voices and their feelings as accurately as possible. It is to them that the book is dedicated.

PC Bristol
MG Aberystwyth
PM Cheltenham

June 1997

1 • Introduction
The Changing Face of Rural Wales

Researching Welsh rural life

It is now almost fifty years since the publication of the book *Life in a Welsh Countryside*, based on Alwyn D. Rees's study of local life in the Montgomeryshire parish of Llanfihangel. This ethnographic study of the culture of one area of rural Wales, undertaken between 1939 and 1946, played a pivotal role in shaping the development of rural community studies in the post-war period, leading to a series of similar studies in other parts of the Welsh countryside between 1945 and 1950 – in Cardiganshire by Jenkins and Jones, the Llŷn Peninsula by Jones Hughes, and Merioneth by Owen (published together in Davies and Rees, 1962). These studies – which might be referred to as the 'Aberystwyth school' of community studies – attempted to explore local life from within, being carried out by researchers who were familiar with local ways of life and possessed knowledge of the study communities through their common roots and language. They were undertaken during a time of creeping change in the Welsh countryside, as many aspects of rural life were becoming increasingly drawn into wider-scale processes of economic and social restructuring. Some of these researchers, though, expressed their own value judgements about such changes, with modernization viewed as detrimental. Rees (1950), for example, in the final paragraph of his book, complained of the threat of urbanization to life in his study parish, and the potential weakening of strong networks of kith and kin, and sense of place:

> The failure of the urban world to give its inhabitants status and significance in a functioning society, and their consequent disintegration into formless masses of rootless nonentities, should make us humble in planning a new life for the countryside. The completeness of the traditional rural society ... and its capacity to give the individual a sense of belonging, are phenomena that might well be pondered by all who seek a better social order. (Rees, 1950, 170)

In addition to the 'Aberystwyth school' of rural community studies, two other pieces of research exploring life in the Welsh countryside were undertaken during this immediate post-war period. The first was carried out by Frankenberg (1957) in a border village in north-east Wales, while the second by Emmett (1964) in an area of north-west Wales. However, the two researchers involved in these projects were not locals to their study areas. Instead, their research of rural life was from without, although each spent long periods of time in these areas. As outsiders they tended to highlight a number of different aspects of local life from those in the 'insider' studies. Frankenberg, for example, placed less emphasis on the role of the church, and more on the position of the football club, local government and the carnival in local community life.

While each of these research projects has demonstrated a rich tapestry of local life in these parts of rural Wales, by the late 1960s and early 1970s the general approaches and methodologies associated with these community studies began to receive considerable criticism from a growing number of sociologists (see Bell and Newby, 1971). The main focus of such criticisms concerned the ways in which researchers treated their study communities as self-sufficient, self-contained and unchanging entities, with little consideration given to class structure, internal tensions and conflict (see Wright, 1992). As such, with the odd exception – see Emmett (1982a, b) – detailed studies of localized life in rural Wales generally lost favour with many researchers during the 1970s and 1980s. More recently, though, there have been calls for a reassessment of the value of these early community studies (see Lewis, 1985) and a small number of studies have been conducted which have explored in some detail aspects of local life in the Welsh countryside – with the work of Bowie (1993) in Gwynedd, Day and Murdoch (1993) in the Ithon Valley and Jones (1992) in Cwmrheidol. These more recent 'community studies', though, have tended to place more emphasis on change and conflict in the Welsh countryside, associated with a range of social, cultural and economic local and wider issues. Indeed, the period since the early Welsh rural community studies were undertaken has been one of considerable restructuring for many parts of rural Wales.

Changing rural Wales[1]

Many areas of rural Wales have witnessed dramatic processes of restructuring in their local economies in the post-war period. The role of agriculture and other primary industries has declined considerably, while manufacturing, and particularly service-sector employment have become much more dominant in local labour markets over the last twenty or so years. The growth of these sectors of employment, though, has been geographically uneven, concentrated in the more accessible parts of the countryside, and particularly the eastern areas. Furthermore, new jobs in the service sector have tended to be characterized by low-quality work, which has been generally aimed at and taken up by women. This employment growth has also failed to raise levels of incomes above national means, with the county of Powys, for example, recording both one of the lowest rates of unemployment and lowest levels of average income in Britain in the early 1990s.

The provision of essential services has also witnessed considerable restructuring over the last few decades. Public transport services, for example, have contracted, with rail services, following first Beeching in the 1960s and cut-backs during the build-up to privatization in the early 1990s, no longer providing everyday transport links in most parts of rural Wales. Likewise Bell and Cloke (1991) have highlighted the decline in rural bus services in the period since deregulation of the industry in the early 1980s. Smaller rural settlements have also witnessed a decline in a range of public-sector services and retail facilities, linked to public-sector restructuring and key settlement policies, and the growth of key retail outlets in larger towns. Finally, in terms of service provision, rural Wales has witnessed both the rapid expansion of council housing in all but a few villages in the immediate decades of the post-war period, and more recently the sell-off of much of this stock to tenants. Indeed, as in other areas of rural Britain, housing markets in many parts of the Welsh countryside are now dominated by the private sector generally, and owner-occupation in particular.

Perhaps the most dramatic change affecting areas of rural Wales in the post-war period, though, has been the reversal of population decline, which had been a feature of Welsh rural life for the first sixty to seventy years of this century. Indeed, population decline and its associated problems were seen by policy-makers as the key issue facing areas of mid-Wales in the 1950s and early 1960s, leading to the establishment of a government-funded development agency (now known as the Development Board for Rural Wales). By the 1970s and early 1980s, statistical evidence from the Censuses of Population was pointing to population increases in many parts of rural Wales, growth rates which continued over the latter years of the 1980s. However, while this reversal of rural population decline has been welcomed by many commentators, these aggregate figures of population growth mask a continued net out-movement of many younger residents from the Welsh country-side, in search of improved employment and higher education opportunities (see Edwards et al., 1992; Milbourne, 1993). Moreover, population growth has been associated with an in-movement of outside groups into Welsh villages, leading to dramatic processes of localized social, and in many cases, cultural recomposition. The scale of this in-migration, particularly during the late 1980s (the population of rural Wales increased by 37,000 persons between 1981 and 1991) and its nature, characterized by a large proportion of English groups (across this same period there was an increase of 47,000 English-born residents), has led to wide-scale concerns about the survival of ways of life, cultures and the Welsh language in parts of the rural Wales (see Day, 1989; Prys Davies, 1989; Carter, 1992). In these parts of the Welsh-speaking countryside, this large-scale in-movement has resulted in consider-able cultural tensions and conflicts within individual communities, and wider-scale protests about the changing composition of the Welsh rural population.

Considerable caution needs to be exercised however when discussing such processes of restructuring at a general level, given that such changes have impacted on different areas of rural Wales in many different ways. Indeed, it is possible to view the Welsh countryside as characterized by considerable internal heterogeneity in a number of important ways. Earlier studies of rural Wales and its communities, for example, have tended to emphasize the different physical geographies of the Welsh countryside, particularly the distinctions between upland and lowland parts, which have acted, and continue to act, to problematize development in some of the western areas and north–south transport links. In economic terms, rural Wales contains local labour-market areas which are character-ized by both the highest and lowest rates of unemployment in

Britain – lowest in the more accessible, eastern areas, highest in the remoter north-west and south-west parts. Finally, a number of commentators have pointed to important political and cultural differences within rural Wales. Voting patterns in the 1992 General Election, for example, have pointed to key political cleavages between the four western constituencies in which Plaid Cymru secured majorities, the eastern border areas where Liberal and Conservative support was stronger, and the southern peri-urban areas of south Wales which tended to return Labour politicians to London. Indeed, Osmond's (1985) description of Wales as a 'fractured and fragmented country' remains equally true of its rural areas in the 1990s, while Balsom (1985) has translated voting patterns into a threefold geographical breakdown of political and cultural identity in rural Wales which serves to highlight important identity facets within the Welsh countryside.

Lifestyles in the Welsh countryside

It is in the context of these key processes of economic restructuring, social and cultural recomposition and shifting service provision that the research for this present volume has been undertaken. Our study of Lifestyles in Rural Wales, aimed to paint a picture of life in selected areas of the Welsh countryside in the early 1990s and to place this picture in a context of changing policies and opportunities. The research was funded by three government organizations active in rural Wales – the Welsh Office, the Development Board for Rural Wales (DBRW) and the Welsh Development Agency (WDA) – which wished to compare the situation in parts of rural Wales with that in selected areas of rural England being studied in a larger research project – Lifestyles in Rural England (see Cloke et al., 1994). Lifestyles in Rural Wales ran from 1991 to 1993, and followed on from initial pilot work undertaken in two areas centred on Corris and Llangammarch Wells in 1990 (a summary of this research is provided in Cloke and Davies, 1992. See also Figures 6.2 and 6.3.)

The research involved interviews with 250 households and a range of key actors in each of four areas of the Welsh countryside – Betws-y-coed in Gwynedd, Devil's Bridge in Ceredigion, the Tanat Valley on the Montgomeryshire/Glyndŵr border, and the

Teifi Valley on the Carmarthen/Ceredigion border – resulting in an overall sample of around 1,000 households (more detailed background information about each study area is provided in appendix 1). The selection of these areas was, in part, intended to ensure that they were distributed throughout rural Wales, and also that they were located evenly between the areas of jurisdiction of the DBRW and WDA. Thus, Betws-y-coed is located solely within the WDA's northern area, Devil's Bridge is wholly within the DBRW area, and both the Tanat Valley and Teifi Valley study areas represent crossborder zones between the two organizations (see Figure 1.1). Apart from this selection criterion, the study areas are not characterized by any particular problems or policy response. Indeed, the idea behind the research was, and remains, that it could have been carried out in almost any part of rural Wales.

Structured interviews were carried out with each of the 250 households in each area which were systematically sampled from the latest electoral registers. Interviews lasted between one-and-a-half and two-and-a-half hours and covered a number of key issues relating to lifestyles in the 1990s countryside, including employment and income, housing, social change, service provision and perceptions of local life. The interview format included a large number of closed questions which related to the more tangible aspects of life in rural Wales and some more in-depth, open-ended questions which probed for the perceptions and experiences of respondents concerning a range of issues. Given the importance of the Welsh language in our study areas, almost all interviews were conducted by Welsh-speaking researchers and, where necessary, responses provided through the medium of Welsh were translated to English.

In addition to our survey of around 1,000 resident households, a range of background information on each study area was obtained through semi-structured interviews with community council clerks and other key actors in the locality. Planning officers were also contacted for details of policy initiatives in the areas included within the research. The open-ended comments provided by our respondents and key interview contacts were recorded verbatim by the interviewer and provide a valuable source of opinion on the nature of, and problems associated with, living in rural Wales. Throughout the book we have attempted wherever possible to interconnect tabulations derived from numeric data with passages of qualitative text

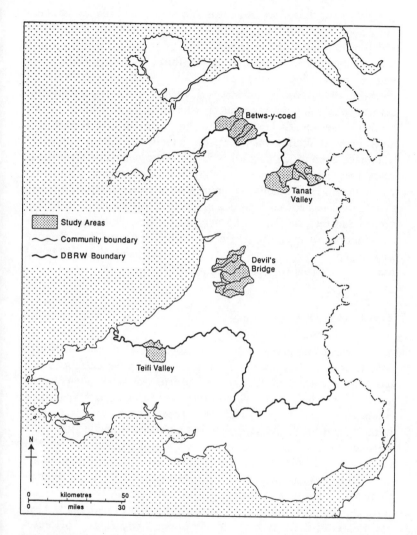

Figure 1.1: Location of the study areas.

derived from these more unstructured sections of the interviews. There are two aims here. First, it is important to allow the voices of rural people to be heard in academic and policy-related studies of rural life.[2] Secondly, the categories by which our respondents discuss the problems of rural life are often more complex and 'messy' than those prescribed in academic and policy studies. Throughout the book we have tried to structure the chapters in ways which reflect some of this complexity.

In summary then, the Lifestyles in Rural Wales research represents a comprehensive study of rural life and lifestyles in Wales in the early 1990s. We would however wish to stress three important caveats concerning the research on which this book is based. First, the 1,000 households in our survey should not be seen as representative of rural Wales as a whole, but merely as indicative of wider situations. Second, although it is important to compare between our study areas, we recognize that there exists considerable variation within these areas. Finally, by employing a household-based survey, this study has neglected particular groups, for example travelling groups and the homeless, who may not be household-based in any conventional manner. While we are not attempting to downplay such groups, we recognize that other research methodologies would need to be utilized to focus on them.

The structure of the book

Although our interpretation of information gathered from the household interviews has been constrained partly by the categories and questions included in the survey format, we have attempted to structure the main body of the book around categories and wider headings which reflect people's own reporting of significant issues in their local areas. As such, our interpretation highlights the ways in which local residents interconnected sets of material issues – for example, population change, employment, housing, service provision and so on – with the perceptions and experiences of life in their local area. It also allows for a discussion of wider processes of restructuring and the ways in which such processes have been experienced differently by residents in our study areas. This interpretative approach is reflected in the presentation of our findings, with individual chapters intermixing both qualitative text and tabulations of numerical information.

The remaining part of this introductory chapter sets out the structure of the individual chapters within this book.

Chapter 2 presents an exploration of issues relating to Welsh identity and culture in our study areas, in which our findings are positioned within the wider context of a growing literature on identity, or more accurately identities, in Wales. The chapter suggests that an understanding of changing notions of Welshness is crucial to readings of population change in areas of the Welsh countryside, and the ways in which such changes result in sets of tensions, conflicts and protest. Here, attention is given to the interplay between different scales of belonging and identity – between national constructs of Welshness and Englishness, and between different facets of Welshness within areas of rural Wales.

The interlinkages between population change and socio-cultural recomposition, and restructuring of local housing markets are considered in chapter 3. Here attention is given to a range of housing-based issues, linked to both the structure of, and the competition for, housing in the countryside. Individual sections of this chapter therefore focus on the changing nature of housing provision and conditions, access to local housing markets, housing need and the potential for socio-cultural conflict surrounding changes in such housing markets.

Employment issues in the four study areas are examined in chapter 4, in which attention is given to changing patterns of employment, underemployment and unemployment in rural Wales. Such changes are also linked with the efforts of development agencies such as the Development Board for Rural Wales and the Welsh Development Agency to create new job opportunities, and attention is given to the ways in which employment experiences and opportunities vary according to gender, age and ethnicity.

In chapter 5, we consider some key changes in rural accessibility, highlighting issues of car ownership, public transport provision and local service provision in our four study areas, and these changes are set against the broader background of transport shifts in Wales and Britain more generally. The chapter identifies problems experienced by particular 'non-mobile' groups in rural Wales, and links these problems with the different experiences of isolation which were expressed to us by our respondents.

Some of our most dramatic findings relate to the incidence of poverty amongst households in rural Wales. These findings, which are presented in chapter 6, highlight the juxtaposition of wealth and poverty in these areas of rural Wales, and aim to challenge mythical notions of 'rural idyll' which are so often ingrained in such places. In this chapter we also explore the ways in which poverty, deprivation and marginalization are experienced by some residents and perceived by many others in our study areas.

In the last findings chapter, chapter 7, we explore the ways in which rural lifestyles in Wales are wrapped up with ideas about and experiences of community, and with the importance of living in a countryside environment. Here we suggest that certain rural residents live their lives according to some imagined community and environmental attributes rather than the material conditions of their existence. What is particularly interesting here is that these imagined attributes differ widely within particular places, and that these differences themselves can lead to important social and cultural conflicts.

Finally, chapter 8 draws this wide-ranging study of Welsh rural lifestyles together, through an assessment of the various opportunities and experiences associated with living in the 1990s Welsh countryside. Problems relating to aspects of such lifestyles are cross-referenced with a range of existing policies in these areas, and here attention is given to the recently published Welsh Rural White Paper. In this chapter, we also recognize that an individual piece of contract research, such as Lifestyles in Rural Wales, does not end with the submission of the final report, and so we finish the book with an account of how various groups – within academic and policy environments – have reacted to our approaches and key findings.

Notes

[1] The definition of rural Wales is somewhat problematic. When we speak of rural Wales in a general context, we refer to those pre-1995 District Councils characterized as 'remote rural' in Cloke's and Edwards's (1986) Index of Rurality. In some chapters, however, the spatial area referred to by the term will vary depending on the type and source of data used. Thus in some cases 'rural Wales' means the area under the jurisdiction of the Development Board for Rural Wales (DBRW), and in others it means the pre-1995 county councils of Dyfed, Gwynedd and Powys. Some statistics are collected for the areas designated for receipt of EU structural funds under Objective 5b, while others refer to travel-to-work areas. In these latter cases where we use data restricted to a specific area, we will always specify the area covered. The different uses and meanings of the term 'rural Wales' in the book are not due to inconsistencies on our part, but

occur because different kinds of data are available at different spatial scales covering a different geographical area.

[2] However, we recognize here the power of the researcher and author as a gatekeeper of these voices, selecting which will and which will not be included in our findings.

References

Balsom, D. (1985) 'The three Wales model', in J. Osmond (ed.), *The National Question Again*, Gomer Press, Llandysul.

Bell, P. and Cloke, P. (1991) 'Deregulation and rural bus services: a study in rural Wales', *Environment and Planning A*, 23, 107-26.

Bowie, F. (1993) 'Wales from within: conflicting interpretations of Welsh identity', in S. Macdonald (ed.), *Inside European Identities*, Berg, Oxford.

Carter, H. (1988) *Immigration and the Welsh Language*, Court of the National Eisteddfod of Wales.

Cloke, P. and Davies, L. (1992) 'Deprivation and lifestyles in rural Wales', I: 'Towards a cultural dimension', *Journal of Rural Studies*, 8, 349-59.

Cloke, P. and Edwards, G. (1986) 'Rurality in England and Wales 1981: a replication of the 1971 index', *Regional Studies*, 20 (4), 289-306.

Cloke, P., Milbourne, P. and Thomas, C. (1994) *Lifestyles in Rural England*, Rural Development Commission, London.

Day, G. (1989) '"A million on the move"? Population change and rural Wales', *Contemporary Wales*, 2, 137-59.

Day, G. and Murdoch, J. (1993) 'Locality and community: coming to terms with place', *Sociological Review*, 82-111.

Edwards, B., Roberts, G., Davies, L. and Davies, K. (1992) *The Economic and Social Circumstances of Young People Living in Rural Wales: Trawsfynydd, Gwynedd*, a report to the Development Board for Rural Wales, Newtown.

Emmett, I. (1964) *A North Wales Village: A Social Anthropological Study*, Routledge and Kegan Paul, London.

Emmett, I. (1982a) 'Fe godwn ni eto: stasis and change in a Welsh industrial town', in A. Cohen, (ed.), *Belonging: Identity and Social Organisation in British Rural Cultures*, Manchester University Press, Manchester.

Emmett, I. (1982b) 'Place, community and bilingualism in Blaenau Ffestiniog', ibid.

Frankenberg, R. (1957) *Village on the Border*, Cohen and West, London.

Jenkins, D. (1960) 'Aberporth', in E. Davies and A. Rees (eds.), *Welsh*

Rural Communities, University of Wales Press, Cardiff.

Jones, E. (1960) 'Tregaron', ibid.

Jones, N. (1992) *Living in Rural Wales*, Gomer Press, Llandysul.

Jones Hughes, T. (1960) 'Aberdaron', in E. Davies, and A. Rees (eds.), *Welsh Rural Communities*, University of Wales Press, Cardiff.

Lewis, G. (1985) 'Welsh rural community studies: retrospect and prospect', *Cambria*, 13 (1), 27–40.

Milbourne P. (1993) *The Dynamics of the Housing Market in Rural Wales*, unpublished Ph.D. thesis, University of Wales, Aberystwyth.

Osmond, J. (1988) *The Divided Kingdom*, Constable, London.

Owen, T (1960) 'Chapel and community in Glan-llyn, Merioneth', in E. Davies and A. Rees (eds.), *Welsh Rural Communities*, University of Wales Press, Cardiff.

Prys Davies, Lord (1989) 'Welsh rural communities', *Hansard*, 19 April, 836–60.

Rees, A. (1950) *Life in a Welsh Countryside*, University of Wales Press, Cardiff (1961 edn).

Appendix 1: The Study Areas[1]

The *Betws-y-coed study area* is located in an area of Gwynedd which includes the town of Betws-y-coed and the villages of Dolwyddelan, Penmachno and Ysbyty Ifan. The area is also situated within the Snowdonia National Park and, as such, is subject to a series of restrictive planning policies which aim to protect and enhance the local landscape and limit new development to that deemed necessary for local areas. The study area has witnessed a great deal of population in-movement over recent years, with the 1991 Census indicating that 10 per cent of persons had moved to their place of residence between 1990 and 1991. The area is also attractive to tourists and holiday-makers and this is evident within the local economy and housing markets. In fact second and holiday homes comprise one in five of all properties in the area and tourism represents a key part of service sector employment (which generally accounts for seven out of ten working residents). The Betws-y-coed area is popular with professional and managerial workers – accounting for around one-fifth of persons in employment – who tend to commute to nearby coastal towns. The local housing market is dominated by private ownership, accounting for 73 per cent of households, with 16 per cent renting from private landlords and a further 12 per cent of households residing in social rental accommodation. Finally, the Welsh language remains strong in this area of rural Wales, with the 1991 Census recording six out of ten residents speaking Welsh.

The *Devil's Bridge study area* consists of an area of Ceredigion situated to the east of Aberystwyth and includes the villages of Bronant, Capel Bangor, Cwmystwyth, Devil's Bridge, Penrhyn-coch, Ponterwyd, Pontrhydfendigaid, Pont-rhyd-y-groes and Ysbyty Ystwyth. The local labour market is dominated by the university town of Aberystwyth and service sector occupations, which account for two-thirds of all employment in the area. Around half of all workers are involved in professional, managerial or non-manual work, although 18 per cent of persons remain employed within the farming industry. The area has witnessed large-scale population in-movement over recent years, with 8 per cent of households moving to their present residence between 1990 and 1991. The level of owner-occupation in the Devil's Bridge area is the highest amongst our areas, accounting for 83 per cent of all households, with 12 per cent in private rented dwellings and a further 5 per cent of households living in social rental accommodation. While the area is popular with tourists, leisure home ownership makes up only 7 per cent of the local housing stock. Finally, even though parts of this area have historically been relatively anglicized, particularly since the establishment of a university in Aberystwyth, around 56 per cent of residents were Welsh-speaking at the 1991 Census point.

The *Tanat Valley study area* is situated in an area of north Montgomeryshire and south Glyndŵr which includes the villages of Hirnant, Llangynog, Llanrhaeadr-ym-Mochnant, Pen-y-bont-fawr and Pengarnedd, and the eastern parts of this area are located close to the English border. Although the Tanat Valley shows much similarity with the other areas in that it has witnessed considerable population in-movement over recent years, the local labour market is less dominated by the service sector – which accounts for around half of all workers – and self-employment, predominantly associated with farming, is particularly strong, accounting for 41 per cent of persons in employment. Furthermore, only 14 per cent of workers are engaged in professional and managerial occupations, with these jobs located mainly in the nearby towns of Oswestry, Shrewsbury and Welshpool. The local housing market is dominated by private ownership, accounting for 62 per cent all households, although private rental, again linked in the farming industry, appears more important than the social rental sector (23 per cent and 15 per cent of households respectively were living in these tenures). Slightly less than one in ten properties were in second or holiday home ownership. Finally, even though this area is characterized by its 'border country' location, the Welsh language remains strong, particularly in the western parts, being spoken by 54 per cent of all residents in 1991.

The *Teifi Valley study area* is located in an area to the east of Newcastle Emlyn in south-west Ceredigion and north Carmarthen and includes the villages of Llandysul, Llandyfriog, Llanfihangel-ar-arth, Llangeler and

Llanwenog. The area has been characterized by considerable population in-movement over recent years, with around 8 per cent of residents moving to their present address in the one year prior to the 1991 Census. The local labour market is characterized by a relatively high rate of unemployment (11 per cent of adult residents) and a low proportion of workers in profes-sional and managerial occupations (9 per cent), and while the service sector accounts for around half of all occupations, a further 19 per cent of workers are engaged in farming-related employment. Private ownership represents the tenure of around three-quarters of all households, with the social rental and private rental sectors making up 17 per cent and 9 per cent of dwellings respectively. The area contains relatively few leisure homes, making up only 4 per cent of the total housing stock. Finally, the Teifi Valley is characterized by the highest rate of Welsh-language usage amongst our four areas, with 64 per cent of residents speaking Welsh in 1991.

Notes

[1] All figures included within this appendix are taken from the 1991 Census of Population.

2 • Social and Cultural Issues in Rural Wales

Changing cultures in the Welsh countryside

Issues of Welsh identity, culture and language represent important aspects of changing lifestyles in rural Wales in the 1990s. With an influx of new groups into many areas over recent years, considerable processes of social and cultural recomposition have taken place. Milbourne (1993), for example, has reported that around 37,000 more people were living in rural Wales in 1991 than was the case in 1981, which represents a 6 per cent growth in the overall rural population. The vast majority of this growth has been associated with an in-movement of outside groups, with many relocating from areas of England (by 1991, 30 per cent of the rural population had been born in England, an increase of almost one-third over the 1980s). However, this overall growth of 37,000 people also masks a continued net out-movement of younger residents from many areas of the Welsh countryside in search of improved lifestyle opportunities.

These processes of selective in- and out-migrations have tended to impact negatively on the use of the Welsh language in many rural communities. While the number of rural residents speaking Welsh increased slightly over the 1980s through the increased support of a range of both public and private bodies in Wales, the proportion of Welsh-speakers in rural areas in 1991 stood at 42 per cent, compared with 46 per cent of residents ten years earlier. In fact, in only two districts – Arfon and Dwyfor – did the proportion of Welsh-speakers constitute more than two-thirds of the overall population (in contrast to the situation in 1981 when four districts recorded such proportions of Welsh-speakers), and Welsh-speakers comprised the majority of the population in only five other districts – Dinefwr, Meirionnydd, Ynys Môn, Ceredigion and Carmarthen.

Such population changes, together with an increasing influence of Anglo-American cultural norms, have led some commentators to talk about a crisis of Welsh identity and culture for many residents in rural Wales (Osmond, 1987). However, caution needs to be exercised when referring to Welsh 'culture' and 'identity', given that such words are attached to a multitude of meanings by different persons. Bowie (1993), for example, has pointed to the ways in which outside constructs of Welsh identity and culture tend to simplify a reality of internal competing understandings of Welshness:

> Wales presents to the rest of the world a coherent picture of cultural self-sufficiency and a firm sense of identity. What outsiders see, however, is not so much Wales as their own reflection, or stereotypes of Welshness, the Wales of the Celtist imagination. As one begins to penetrate beyond this refracted image of Welshness, not least by learning the Welsh language, the unproblematic and monolithic nature of Welsh identity begins to fragment. One is left not so much with a coherent notion of Welshness . . . as with a sense of many conflicting and interlocking definitions of identity which actively compete for symbolic space and public recognition. (pp.168–9)

Such conflicting definitions of Welshness have been highlighted by a number of authors over recent years. Aaron et al. (1993), for example, have attempted to incorporate the voices of Welsh women within national constructs of identity, while Williams (1995) has pointed to the neglect of black identities in mainstream notions of Welshness. In addition, Balsom (1985) has suggested that it is possible to identify a geographical breakdown of Welsh culture and identity – what he terms a 'three Wales model' – on the basis of recent voting patterns, with this model pointing to two important 'regions of identity' in the Welsh countryside: *Y Fro Gymraeg* – the Welsh-speaking heartland – comprising the western parts of mid-Wales and much of the county of Gwynedd, which is characterized by a strong use of the Welsh language, a distinctive Welsh identity, and nationalistic politics (each of its four constituencies elected Plaid Cymru MPs in 1992); and British Wales, consisting of the eastern border areas of Monmouth, Powys and Clwyd, and Pembrokeshire in the south-west, where the Welsh language is spoken by relatively few residents, identity is characterized more by Britishness than Welshness, and independent/conservative politics tend to dominate (five of its sixteen constituencies elected the only Conservative MPs in Wales in 1992).

While population in-movement has impacted on most parts of rural Wales, it has been largely within *Y Fro Gymraeg* – the Welsh-speaking heartland – that an in-movement of outside, predominantly English groups has resulted in considerable cultural changes, tensions and conflicts. In its most obvious guise, much of this change and conflict is clearly linked to an influx of groups who do not, at least initially, speak Welsh, the common language of every-day interactions (see Aitchison and Carter, 1991; Day, 1989). Indeed, the dramatic linguistic impacts of such population changes in Welsh-speaking rural communities have led Osmond (1987) to talk of 'a sudden and deepening crisis for the future of the Welsh language and for the wider cultural identity of Wales as a whole' (p.118), while a member of the House of Lords – Lord Prys Davies (1989) – has suggested that many Welsh rural communities are now no longer in a position to assimilate any additional outsider residents within their cultural fabric.

Within these situations of population change and an in-movement of English groups, we see an interaction of competing (national-scale) identities of Englishness and Welshness, with key facets of Englishness viewed by some Welsh-speaking residents as an import-ant threat to everyday lifestyles – a 'significant other' (Cohen, 1985). Indeed, Cohen has suggested that it is in these situations of interaction with 'others' that identities are shaped and cultural distinctiveness becomes most apparent. What is also visible in such interactions between local and newcomer, insider and outsider, Welsh and English is a juxtaposition of different scales of identity, as components of national (Welsh) identity become intertwined with more localized identities bound up with strong feelings of belonging and cultural distinctiveness (see Emmett, 1982). Indeed, we would wish to suggest that it is the interplay between these different scales or facets of Welshness that is crucial to any understanding of cultural change and conflict in areas of rural Wales. That is to say, it is not possible to read localized issues without reference to interactions between wider-scale, and particularly national-level constructs of Englishness and Welshness, while these wider-scale identities of Welshness and Englishness can be seen to be played out in local arenas of interaction. Indeed, as Cohen (1982, 13) has commented, these larger-scale identities represent merely 'empty receptacles which are filled with local and particular experience'.

However, Williams (1985) has suggested that such constructions of Englishness as threat and 'significant other' are often associated with specific notions of English identity which may act to homogenize a diverse range of individual identities associated with English newcomers. Individual identities of the English can become subsumed within wider notions of Englishness, bound up with images of ruling England and the apparatus of the English state (ibid.), and thus, for those English in-movers not holding on to such narrow constructions of Englishness, individual identities may become initially conflated with notions of Englishness as threat amongst many (Welsh-speaking) rural residents.

The chapter now moves on to explore these issues of language, culture and competing constructs of identity in the context of our research. The next section explores the role played by Welsh culture and the Welsh language in our four study areas. The chapter then explores issues of cultural change and conflict in these areas of rural Wales.

Welsh language and culture

In each of our study areas the Welsh language and associated culture(s) featured prominently in everyday rural lifestyles. In terms of language use, an average of half of all residents claimed to be fluent speakers of Welsh, ranging from 41.3 per cent of persons in the Devil's Bridge study area to 61.2 per cent of Betws-y-coed residents. In addition, the household survey revealed that a further 10 per cent of residents were 'less than fluent' Welsh-speakers, and a similar proportion of persons were currently learning the language (table 2.1). While most of such learners were primary school children who were being taught through the medium of Welsh, our survey did indicate a significant minority of English in-movers who were attending language classes, and this was particularly true in the Devil's Bridge study area. However, it remains the case that each study area has witnessed a dramatic decline in the proportion of residents speaking Welsh over recent years, with non-Welsh-speakers comprising around three out of ten persons across the four areas. Interestingly, Rees's (1950) research indicated that less than 3 per cent of persons in his Llanfihangel parish – situated less than twenty miles from the English border – were unable to speak Welsh. In the Tanat Valley study area, situated less than ten miles from Llanfihangel, the proportion of non-Welsh-speakers was in excess of ten times higher than this figure, at 38 per cent of all residents in 1990–1.

Table 2.1: Welsh-language use by residents (percentages)

	Betws-y-coed	Devil's Bridge	Tanat Valley	Teifi Valley	All
Fluent	61.2	41.3	44.0	53.1	49.9
Less than fluent	6.4	15.1	9.3	11.1	10.4
Learning	8.9	13.1	8.9	10.1	10.2
Non-Welsh-speaking	23.5	30.5	37.8	25.7	29.5

The geography of Welsh-speakers would appear to reflect a west–east, *Y Fro Gymraeg*–British Wales cultural division within rural Wales, with the easterly study area of the Tanat Valley recording the lowest proportion of Welsh-speaking residents. However, in our three westerly study areas considerable variation is evident in the proportions of residents speaking Welsh, and this is particularly the case between Devil's Bridge and the other two areas. In this sense then, while language use in our three study areas would seem to confirm Balsom's regional breakdown of Welsh culture and identity in rural Wales, it is clear that we need to be aware of localized factors. For example, in the case of the Devil's Bridge study area, the presence of a university at Aberystwyth may have been associated with localized processes of anglicization, linked to an in-movement of staff and students from areas of England.

Our interviews with Welsh-speaking residents also explored the use of Welsh in different types of formal and informal environments. In general terms, Welsh appeared to be spoken by greater proportions of residents at home and in leisure arenas than in places of employment. In fact, table 2.2 highlights that an average of just over two-thirds of Welsh-speakers (in this case the category 'Welsh-speaker' includes 'fluent' and 'less than fluent' speakers as well as 'learners') spoke Welsh at home, and three-quarters used the language during times of leisure. It is also clear from this table that the use made of Welsh by Welsh-speakers in the Devil's Bridge area is less pronounced than in the other areas, a phenomenon that may be explained by the higher proportions of 'less than fluent' Welsh-speakers and learners resident in this area.

It is also interesting within any discussion of the Welsh language to explore the use made of Welsh by younger residents. Across our study areas, an average of 57.9 per cent of all children (under sixteen years) were being educated through the medium of Welsh (mainly at primary school level), with over three-quarters of school children in Devil's Bridge being taught through the Welsh language

Table 2.2: Proportions of Welsh-speakers* using the language in home, work** and leisure environments (first two adults in household)

	Betws-y-coed	Devil's Bridge	Tanat Valley	Teifi Valley	All
Home	78.3	55.7	65.8	69.8	67.9
Work	45.7	45.9	47.7	45.4	46.1
Leisure	88.0	65.6	74.2	70.8	74.9

* Welsh-speakers include the categories 'fluent', 'less than fluent' and 'learning' used in table 2.1.
** This table includes adults who are not presently working, which has deflated these figures.

Table 2.3: Proportions of children (under sixteen years) being taught through the medium of Welsh (percentages)

Betws-y-coed	52.6
Devil's Bridge	77.8
Tanat Valley	50.0
Teifi Valley	50.0
All areas	57.9

(table 2.3). Such a finding would appear to point to a continued, or even increased, use of Welsh – in both so-called newcomer and longer-established households – into the near and medium future (although see the later section on language conflicts in schools).

This statistical evidence of the importance of Welsh as an everyday language of interaction in these parts of rural Wales was reinforced through a series of interviews with key actors and local residents in each study area. These interviews pointed to strong localized feelings of Welshness which were generally underpinned by the Welsh language. However, it is important to note that discussion of Welshness and the Welsh language in these interviews was often located in a wider context of social and cultural change within local areas, and particularly an in-movement of outside (English) groups and a creeping Anglicization of much of Welsh rural life. In the commentaries highlighted below, which are taken from interviews with community council clerks in our study areas, it is evident that issues of Welsh language, culture and identity tend to be discussed in relation to a changing Welsh countryside:

[This is a] strong Welsh speaking village – oh yes, I would say so. [There are] English moving in [but] their children can now speak Welsh. [PM: any tensions?] Oh no. (Teifi Valley clerk)

I should imagine that three-quarters of the people would be Welsh-speaking or possibly in excess of that – a fairly informed estimate. [The Welsh] language and culture [are] still quite strong – good response by English-speaking parents to [the] Welsh-language school – twenty youngsters there at present. (Devil's Bridge clerk)

[The] majority of people speak Welsh round here, although I do know Welsh-born people who have lived in Wales all their life who can't speak Welsh. A lot of English have a go at learning Welsh. I've had private lessons and been on courses but I got nowhere. But I'm going to try again. There are a few Welsh Nationalists – we've had two fires ... The people were away on holiday and it was totally gutted – they were English people but they had been living here permanently. (Devil's Bridge clerk)

It is also evident in these and other commentaries provided by clerks that English in-movement to local areas is being discussed in neutral or weakly positive terms – responses which would seem to be at odds with many commentaries provided by residents in our surveys (outlined in the next section of this chapter). Such reactions may be seen to be linked, in part, to the nature of these interviews with clerks, given that each was undertaken by a non-Welsh-speaking researcher. As such, it may be suggested that feelings concerning an influx of English groups may have been diluted for reasons of politeness, with respondents not wishing to criticize a group which included the interviewer. Furthermore, it can also be suggested that these clerks might have constructed themselves as the spokespersons for their communities and so may have produced more 'diplomatic' responses when discussing such issues. In these senses, then, it may be the case that discussions of English in-movement to these areas and its impacts on local social and cultural structures are bound up with Cohen's (1986) ideas of inside and outside constructions of local life and community, in which notions of local community feeling may be acting as a 'public face' for how its members wish to see themselves viewed from the outside.

Experiences of social and cultural change

Reference was made in the introduction of this chapter to a large-scale in-movement of new groups to the Welsh countryside, and the

Table 2.4: Respondents reporting population change over 'recent times' (percentages)

	Yes	No	Don't know
Tanat Valley	80.2	16.4	3.4
Devil's Bridge	77.1	18.8	4.0
Teifi Valley	74.8	20.8	4.4
Betws-y-coed	61.3	31.5	7.3
All areas	73.1	22.0	4.8

Table 2.5: Types of persons moving to the local area over 'recent times' (percentages)

	Betws-y-coed	Devil's Bridge	Tanat Valley	Teifi Valley	All
More immigrants from towns, commuters	65.7	55.9	53.2	31.3	52.3
More retired people	16.3	21.6	24.8	11.3	19.4
Fewer young people	7.3	2.8	9.2	1.9	5.6
Fewer elderly people	0.0	0.5	1.6	1.9	1.9
Fewer people in agriculture	1.1	1.4	2.8	1.9	1.9
Other	9.6	17.8	8.4	51.9	19.9

Table 2.6: Reactions to population changes over recent times (percentages)

	Betws-y-coed	Devil's Bridge	Tanat Valley	Teifi Valley	All
Strongly approve	0.7	2.2	7.3	5.0	3.6
Approve on balance	8.6	5.3	22.0	15.1	11.6
No particular feelings or don't know	25.2	20.4	36.2	40.8	29.1
Disapprove on balance	49.0	12.6	23.2	26.8	24.2
Strongly disapprove	16.6	59.4	11.3	12.3	31.0

socio-cultural impacts of such population change. Our interviews in the four study areas explored residents' perceptions of these changes, both in terms of the composition of new groups moving to these areas of rural Wales and reactions to such in-movement. It is clear from these interviews that such population growth, linked predominantly to an in-movement of outside groups, also represented a key feature of changing local life in our study areas. Table 2.4, for example, highlights that around three-quarters of residents recognized recent population change in their areas, with such recognition ranging from 61.3 per cent of respondents in Betws-y-coed to 80.2 per cent of those living in the Tanat Valley study area.

By far the most frequently cited group of persons mentioned by respondents as associated with local population change was those moving in from outside areas, particularly people relocating in from urban areas, either to commute to outside labour markets or to retire in the Welsh countryside (table 2.5). Indeed, in three areas – Betws-y-coed, Devil's Bridge and the Tanat Valley – in excess of three-quarters of all respondents mentioned that these groups had moved into their local area, with the large number of 'other' responses in the Teifi Valley sample resulting from more overt references to an English, rather than immigrant, in-movement. However, while it is clear that dominant perceptions of change are linked to an in-movement of outside groups to each area, table 2.5 also indicates that an out-migration of certain younger rural residents remains an issue for some residents, particularly in the Betws-y-coed and Tanat Valley study areas.

While our research has indicated a widespread awareness of population change over recent years in each area, particularly associated with an in-movement of outside groups, reactions to such change appeared to vary markedly both within and between study areas. Indeed, it is evident from table 2.6 that these different experiences of population change appear, on the one hand, to reinforce, while on the other to contradict, Balsom's *Y Fro Gymraeg*–British Wales identity divide discussed earlier. An average of 55.2 per cent of respondents across our four study areas stated that they disapproved of recent population changes in their local areas, with such feelings of disapproval appearing most intense in two of our study areas located in Welsh-speaking areas – Betws-y-coed and Devil's Bridge, where 65.6 per cent and 72.0 per cent of residents respectively felt that these changes were detrimental to the local area – and least strong in the Tanat Valley study area (34.5 per cent). Our research, however, also reveals considerable differences of reaction to population change in Welsh-speaking parts, most notably between the Teifi Valley and the other two *Y Fro Gymraeg* areas. Here, in this strongly Welsh-speaking study area, only four out of ten residents expressed any feelings of disapproval to population change and an in-movement of English groups.

Our research also explored in greater depth perceptions and experiences of population change in local areas with our respondents.

Amongst those residents who expressed disapproval of recent changes, discussion tended to be dominated by references to an influx of 'outsiders', 'foreigners' and 'the English', which was perceived as constituting a significant threat to the survival of the Welsh language and rural ways of life. Indeed, within many of these interviews, it is evident that English in-movement is being labelled as a collective threat, which warrants general disapproval and, at times, active resistance. The three comments outlined below, from Welsh-speaking residents in Devil's Bridge and Betws-y-coed, are particularly illustrative of such perceived threats:

> There has been a substantial increase in retired English people. They come and destroy the Welshness of the Welsh countryside and are detrimental to the culture of our society' (1222, Betws-y-coed – four-figure numbers following this quote and subsequent quotes throughout the book refer to our own coding and storage of interview material. The place name refers to the study area in which the interview was carried out.)

> English immigrants have slowly increased over the years. These people are ruining the Welsh identity and are mostly killing the Welsh language. (1112, Betws-y-coed)

> Lots of English have moved in to retire and look for jobs ... I don't like so many English in the area. It's a shame they picked this place. (2225, Devil's Bridge)

In other commentaries provided by respondents it is possible to detect a set of more specific attributes attached to some English in-movers which may lead to their being constructed as a significant threat. Certain English newcomers were accused frequently of trying to take over village affairs, and importing perceived English ways of life – linked to economic power, business-like attitudes, and, at times, colonial ideologies – into the Welsh(-speaking) countryside. Other groups of English in-migrants, however, were seen as unwilling to integrate into mainstream village life, and were criticized for 'living as if they were still in England'. Again, such feelings against these English newcomers appeared to be most intense in those areas where the Welsh language was strong:

> There is [general] antagonism if people move in and don't appreciate and respect perhaps the traditions and the Welsh language. (Betws-y-coed clerk)

Lots move from the south-east. [They] sell their houses at a huge profit and buy a bigger place in Wales. These people are arrogant, selfish bastards who become very smug and have no sympathy at all. They want to turn the place into another Surrey. (2196, Devil's Bridge)

Some English come here and act like colonials – talk about us as peasants. (4138, Teifi Valley)

Thus, it can be suggested that some English persons moving to areas of Welsh-speaking rural Wales may be perceived by Welsh-speaking residents as insensitive to local ways of life, importing portfolios of different cultural competences linked to images of English rural life (see Cloke et al., 1997). Other Welsh-speaking residents, though, highlighted the ways in which views of 'the English as threat' became diluted through processes of assimilation and personal interaction between the newcomers and local residents, with the identity of individual in-movers able to be separated from wider threats of cultural change. Indeed, in the following commentary there are close parallels with some of Emmett's findings (1982a, b) from her research in Gwynedd:

English people [are] coming into this area ... [they] affect the culture ... come in with money ... [the] Welsh are nice to them. In principle, I don't want them here, but as human beings I treat them individually. (2097, Devil's Bridge)

The chapter so far has tended to highlight processes of English in-movement to areas of Welsh-speaking rural Wales which have been perceived by many residents as detrimental to the Welsh language and culture in their local areas. Our research findings, though, have also pointed to sets of perceived benefits associated with an in-migration of new groups to study areas. Such beneficial outcomes of in-movement were mentioned mainly by residents in the Tanat Valley and the Teifi Valley areas, where 29 per cent and 20 per cent of respondents respectively perceived these new groups in positive terms (see table 2.5). For these residents, newcomers were viewed frequently as importing a range of skills and financial resources into the local area, strengthening the social and cultural fabric of villages and improving housing which would otherwise remain unoccupied:

[The] Welsh have moved away and the English have come in their place. [I'm] pleased to see some people living here instead of empty houses. (3207, Tanat Valley)

A lot of English [have] moved in and are doing very well financially. If [the] English didn't come in, the place would die – they bring money with them and pay taxes. (3203, Tanat Valley)

The English bring some very good qualities into the area. I am one of them. The advent of the English drift has brought a lot of ideas into the area, especially in the area of craft. (2092, Devil's Bridge)

Symbolic conflicts: housing, education and religion

It can be suggested that in areas of Welsh-speaking rural Wales, where outside processes of change begin to threaten local cultures, certain structural boundaries may become replaced or reinforced by a number of important symbols, around which such change can be resisted and contested (see Cohen, 1985 for a more detailed discussion of such symbolic boundaries). For example, Bowie (1993) has highlighted how the term 'English' can take on meaning beyond the realm of the purely linguistic, to indicate notions of 'outsideness', 'newcomer' and 'non-local'. In some of our interviews with Welsh-speaking respondents, such references were sometimes made to aspects of symbolic boundaries in their discussions of cultural change and conflict in their local areas. An analysis of these responses reveals that three symbols of wider cultural recomposition were most frequently mentioned by these Welsh-speaking residents: housing (the house), education (the school) and religion (the church or chapel).

Of these examples, it is probably housing that has become most commonly and powerfully utilized as a symbol with which to contest and protest against socio-cultural change in Welsh-speaking areas of rural Wales. Over the 1980s, the English-owned house or holiday cottage became both a key symbolic issue and sometimes burning object within the campaign of Meibion Glyndŵr, a 'direct-action' nationalist movement. Indeed, the image of the holiday home ablaze has become a potent icon of resistance and cultural separateness within parts of the Welsh countryside. Furthermore, Cymdeithas Yr Iaith Gymraeg – the Welsh Language Society – has campaigned over recent years on language issues in Wales using both direct and indirect action centred on housing, with calls for a new property act for Wales which will protect many young Welsh-speaking (rural) residents from unequal competition in private housing markets. In these campaigns, it is possible to view a conflation of the economic and the cultural in discussions on housing change and conflict; of economic exploitation of local groups by more affluent in-movers, and a dilution of Welshness and the use made of Welsh as growing numbers of English persons have moved into areas of the Welsh countryside. In some of our own interviews with Welsh-speakers, it is possible to view rural housing being used as a symbol of these wider economic and cultural processes:

A lot of English people have moved in [and are] able to buy homes. [They are] preventing young people from buying homes. [The] village is dying – its people are being driven out. (3029, Tanat Valley)

Affluent English people – especially of retirement age – [have] escalated local prices of housing beyond the means of local people. [The] locality [is] losing its character – local children [are] losing their first language. (4198, Teifi Valley)

Our interviews with residents in these four areas of rural Wales also pointed to education or the school as playing another key symbolic role within local communities, particularly in relation to the composition of classes and the language of education. While it was reported earlier that a majority of children in surveyed households were being educated through the medium of Welsh (see table 2.3), interviews revealed that a small number of parents, predominantly from English in-comer households, were objecting to the designation of Welsh-medium schools in their localities. In certain areas, these objections had led to the formation of a campaign group known as 'Education First', which argues that parents should be allowed to choose the language(s) through which their children are taught, with the preferred (first) language for parents within this group being English. In terms of the membership of this group then, the comment made by one of our Welsh-speaking respondents earlier in the chapter, that some English in-movers wish to 'live as if they were still in England', would appear to hold true. Indeed, in the Teifi Valley the language issue in local schools was seen by several respondents as creating a great deal of tension and conflict. The following comments provide a graphic illustration of how the language of education is clearly linked to wider processes of cultural change and conflict:

> Welsh and English in schools is a very big issue – [the] school is a category A. Three families wanted their children to be taught through English and it was a Welsh-medium school. It caused a big stink and a lot of upset. (4146, Teifi Valley)

> Language at school [is the greatest conflict] – someone up the road had paint thrown on their house. (4138, Teifi Valley)

> We've been Anglicised more, more movement of English-speaking people. [PM: has this caused any tensions?] I wouldn't say tension. I suppose where it is most obvious is in education where we've got a category A school and I'm in the teaching world myself, and that's where you feel the tension greatest. I suppose with Education First . . . creating an awareness of what the problem is. (Devil's Bridge clerk)

Finally, in addition to these interconnections between housing and education, and wider cultural changes, our interviews also highlighted more limited references to religion, and particularly the place of religion (the church or chapel), as taking on a more symbolic role in particular villages. Again, in this final comment it is evident that this particular respondent places considerable importance on the language of religion, with a great deal of tension resulting from any changes to this language:

> [The] new vicar conducts English and bilingual services which we don't attend. There is coffee after the service which we don't attend . . . we want a Welsh church. (4136, Teifi Valley)

Conclusion

In this chapter, we have suggested that recent processes of population movement and social change in areas of the Welsh countryside cannot be understood fully without a consideration of those issues of culture which are bound up with notions of Welshness and the Welsh language. While we would recognize that the snapshot nature of the Lifestyles in Rural Wales research may not represent the best way to investigate issues of cultural change and conflict in our study areas, it has nevertheless been possible to identify a series of competing constructs of identity within these parts of the Welsh countryside. At one level, we have pointed to some national-scale identity conflicts, in which residents moving into Welsh-speaking areas from parts of England have been criticized for 'living as if they were in England' and undermining the very basis of Welsh rural life. Such national-level cultural conflicts though, have tended to be much less pronounced in our Tanat Valley study area – located close to the English border – where historical Welsh–English interactions have diluted wider-scale identity conflicts into more locally based issues.

It is clear from the material presented in this chapter that the Welsh language and associated cultures remain strong in our three westerly study areas, and act as cultural linchpins in everyday local life. However, it is also the case that feelings of Welshness and the proportions speaking Welsh in these areas have been very much diluted by recent processes of population in- and out-movement – as new groups have relocated into these areas, and many younger, Welsh-speaking residents have moved out in search of improved life chances. Indeed, in many of the commentaries provided in the chapter, it has been evident that local ways of life are very often discussed under this shadow of social recomposition, and the shifting balance between Welsh and English (or Anglo-American) cultural norms. This said, our surveys have also uncovered a more positive picture for the future of the Welsh language in these four areas, as at least half of all school children in each area were being taught through the medium of Welsh at the time of our surveys.

References

Aaron, J., Rees, T., Betts, S. and Vincentelli, M. (1994) *Our Sisters' Land: The Changing Identities of Women in Wales*, University of Wales Press, Cardiff.

Aitchison, J. and Carter, H. (1991) 'Rural Wales and the Welsh Language', *Rural History*, 2, 1, 61–79.

Balsom, D. (1985) 'The three Wales model', in J. Osmond (ed.), *The National Question Again: Welsh Political Identity in the 1980s*, Gomer Press, Llandysul.

Bowie, F. (1993) 'Wales from within: conflicting interpretations of Welsh identity', in S. Macdonald (ed.), *Inside European Identities*, Berg, Oxford.

Carter, H. (1988) *Immigration and the Welsh Language*, Court of the National Eisteddfod of Wales.

Cloke, P. Goodwin, M. and Milbourne, P. (1997) 'Inside looking out, outside looking in: different experiences of cultural competence in rural lifestyles', in P. Boyle and K. Halfacree (eds.), *Migration into Rural Areas: Theories and Issues*, Wiley, London.

Cohen, A. (1985) *The Symbolic Construction of Community*, Routledge, London.

Cohen, A. (1986) 'Of symbols and boundaries, or, does Ertie's greatcoat hold the key?', in A. Cohen, (ed.), *Symbolising Boundaries: Identity and Diversity in British Cultures*, Manchester University Press, Manchester.

Cohen, R. (1994) *Frontiers of Identity: The British and the Others*, Macmillan, London.

Day, G. (1989) '"A million on the move"?: population change and rural Wales', *Contemporary Wales*, 2, 137–59.

Edwards, B., Roberts, G., Davies, L. and Davies, K. (1992) *The Economic and Social Circumstances of Young People Living in Rural Wales: Trawsfynydd, Gwynedd*, a report to the Development Board for Rural Wales, Newtown.

Emmett, I. (1982a) 'Fe godwn ni eto: stasis and change in a Welsh industrial town', in A. Cohen (ed.), *Belonging: Identity and Social Organisation in British Rural Cultures*, Manchester University Press, Manchester.

Emmett, I. (1982b) 'Place, community and bilingualism in Blaenau Ffestiniog', ibid.

Milbourne, P. (1993) *The Dynamics of the Housing Market in Rural Wales*, unpublished Ph.D. thesis, University of Wales, Aberystwyth.

Osmond, J. (1987) 'A million on the move?', *Planet*, 62, 114–18.

Prys Davies, Lord (1989) 'Welsh rural communities', *Hansard*, 19 April, 836–60.

Rees, A (1950) *Life in a Welsh Countryside*, University of Wales Press, Cardiff (1961 edn).

Williams, C. (1995) '"Race" and racism: some reflections on the Welsh context', *Contemporary Wales*, 8, 113–32.

Williams, R. (1985) 'Wales and England', in J. Osmond (ed.), *The National Question Again*, Gomer Press, Llandysul.

3 • Housing and Social Change

Introduction

> When you move to an old house in the Welsh countryside, you are taking on more than a nice place to live, in a beautiful landscape. The siting of houses, the materials used to build them, and the people who lived there in the past, are all part of the continuing story of a locality, and a new owner has responsibility to acknowledge this. One way is to try to understand the way of life, past and present, in these old houses, and their relationship with the broader sweep of history – farming ups and downs, the rise and fall of rural industries and crafts, rural depopulation or repopulation by incomers and visitors. (Jones, 1993, 281)

Housing issues and problems in rural Wales cannot be understood solely in relation to aggregate statistics on changing patterns of tenure, conditions, costs and so on. Although these are clearly important factors, housing in the Welsh countryside, as Noragh Jones suggests, is bound up with sets of historical and contemporary social and cultural issues. In this chapter we consider the multifaceted nature of housing change, problems and conflicts in our four study areas. In doing this, we attempt to bring together the material and symbolic aspects of rural housing in a Welsh context. We discuss the changing provision of housing, in relation to issues such as tenure, conditions, the planning system, and housing need, as well as the ways in which housing issues have become interconnected with population flows into and out of these areas of rural Wales. Before going on to consider some of our key findings on rural housing issues, though, it is important to place our own research within a wider context of studies which have explored housing issues in the Welsh and British countryside over recent years.

Rural housing, in both Wales and Britain, has received relatively little attention from rural researchers over recent years. Those studies which have been conducted have tended to remain locked within the realm of single issues, rather than exploring the ways in which rural housing interconnects with other aspects of social, cultural, political and economic change in the Welsh countryside.

For example, during the 1970s several studies focused on the impacts of second homes on selected communities in rural Wales (see Bollom, 1978; Coppock, 1977), while more recently, research has tended to focus on issues of housing need experienced by low-income groups in areas of the Welsh countryside (Tai Cymru, 1990a, b). However, in some of these studies of rural housing need – many of which have been commissioned or carried out by public bodies or community councils – it is possible to identify various linkages between housing issues and problems and processes of socio-cultural change and conflict. Housing, in this sense, comes to represent a channel of entry into and exit from villages in the Welsh countryside, and, as such, brings with it a considerable weight of symbolic baggage; the nature of certain local housing markets permits, even encourages, an in-movement of more affluent, outside groups, while these same markets push many low-income households away in search of more affordable housing options. Such connections between housing issues and wider socio-cultural changes have been stressed by a report produced by Community Action for Social and Economic Development in 1989:

> People who cannot gain access to housing will move away in search of it and the 'forced' displacement of local people in this way inevitably has adverse social and cultural consequences for communities. The importance of kinship and social networks in enabling people to go on living in their own familiar environment must not be dismissed.

The changing state of rural housing

The nature of housing markets in many areas of rural Wales has changed dramatically over recent years. Consecutive pieces of housing legislation introduced by Conservative governments – from the 1980 Housing Act to the recent Housing Act 1996 – have strengthened the traditional role of the private sector as housing provider in the Welsh countryside. Local authorities have witnessed a steady diminution of their interventionist powers in rural housing markets, as council-house building programmes have been slashed and council tenants have been given the right to purchase their properties. The local authority now performs the role of housing enabler, with new social rental housing provided instead by housing associations – albeit at a much a lower level of funding. The effects

Table 3.1: The changing nature of housing construction in rural Wales, 1981-5 and 1986-91

	Percentage of properties completed	
	1981-5	1986-91
Private sector	75.4	84.3
Local authorities/new towns	19.8	5.3
Housing associations	4.9	10.5

Source: Welsh Housing Statistics (1981-92).

of such legislative shifts on construction patterns in rural Wales over the 1980s and early 1990s are highlighted in table 3.1. While the private sector increased its share of overall housing constructions from 75.4 per cent in the early 1980s to around 84.3 per cent between 1986 and 1991, the proportion of new builds provided by local authorities fell from 19.8 to 5.3 per cent across this same period. It is also clear from this table that housing associations' contributions to total new property constructions doubled between 1981-5 and 1986-91, although this sector accounted for only one in ten new completions in the latter period. Indeed, Milbourne (forthcoming) reports that for every new housing-association dwelling provided in rural Wales over the 1980s, two council houses were sold to sitting tenants.

By 1991, owner-occupation accounted for the tenure of seven out of ten of all households in rural Wales, an increase of more than 15 per cent on the situation in 1981 (see table 3.2). Local authority housing, although still the next most dominant housing tenure, witnessed a reduction in its share of the overall rural housing market, from one-quarter of all households in 1981 to only 14.7 per cent of households ten years later. It is also clear from this table that although housing-association provision has increased dramatically over the 1980s, the sector accounted for only 1.7 per cent of all households in 1991. Finally, the stock of private rented dwellings fell slightly between 1981 and 1991, accounting for 11.6 per cent of all households in 1991, although the furnished private-rental properties witnessed a dramatic increase over the 1980s (encouraged mainly by housing legislation).

Over recent years, though, central government has also recognized a set of housing-based problems in many rural areas, linked to free-market housing policies and the strong role of the state in the planning process. With restrictive planning policies operating in

Table 3.2: Changing patterns of tenure in rural Wales, 1981–91

	Percentage of households	
	1981	1991
Owner-occupied	60.6	70.2
Local authorities/new towns	24.5	14.7
Housing associations	0.6	1.7
Private rental – furnished	2.3	3.6
Private rental – unfurnished	7.7	5.3
Rented with job/business	3.3	2.7

Source: Censuses of Population, 1981, 1991.

many areas of (open) countryside, together with increased pressures of demand for rural housing, clauses have been included in recent housing legislation to shelter certain rural housing markets from the full forces of the private market. For example, right-to-buy sales included in the 1980 Housing Act have been restricted within designated rural areas, while such a proposal is included in the government's plans to sell off housing-association properties. Furthermore, the Welsh Office (1989) has recognized problems with providing affordable accommodation in smaller settlements in the countryside, and has introduced an exceptions policy under which small-scale housing developments can be permitted outside designated areas in order to meet local housing need.

While considerable discussion continues over both the level of housing need in rural Wales – not least because local communities have been encouraged to conduct their own 'needs' surveys in order to 'prove' that need exists, and the most effective ways of tackling such identified need – it is clear that the weight of research findings suggests that the structuring of opportunities for affordable rural housing resulting from housing policies of the post-1980 period has presented additional problems for low-income groups in the Welsh countryside. In 1991, for example, some 1,200 households were accepted by local authorities in rural Wales as homeless, a level more than double that recorded in the mid-1980s (Welsh Office, 1986b, 1992), and it can be suggested that this figure represents a significant under-counting of the real homelessness situation in the Welsh countryside. Furthermore, a report commissioned by Tai Cymru (1990b) has estimated that almost 17,000 households were on waiting lists for social rental housing in 1989–90, with this level of housing need again having increased dramatically over the 1980s.

Housing need has emerged as a key issue in the Welsh country-side over recent years. From around the mid-1980s, an increasing number of commentators, organizations and pressure groups began to highlight sets of problems being faced by a number of local groups, linked to the provision of and competition for rural housing. Typically, these problems have concerned a lack of afford-able housing for both rent and purchase, increasing demands on local housing markets for leisure, retirement and commuter homes, local groups being priced out of housing markets, and tight restric-tions on the provision of new housing in the countryside.

Housing and social change

The Lifestyles in Rural Wales research has tended to reinforce the important role played by housing within the Welsh countryside, pointing to a wide-scale recognition of housing change, problems and conflicts amongst local residents. In overall terms, slightly more than half of our respondents reported that important changes had taken place recently in local housing markets (table 3.3), with such perceived changes appearing greatest in the Teifi Valley and Devil's Bridge areas (mentioned by 69.1 per cent and 64.0 per cent of respondents respectively). Reactions to these localized housing changes (highlighted in table 3.4) tended, on the whole, to be neutral or mildly positive in nature, although a majority of respond-ents in the Devil's Bridge area expressed disapproval of recent changes to their local housing market. Such reactions can be seen as linked to two main factors: first, the ways in which housing change is interconnected to wider processes of social and cultural change; and second, a range of localized issues related to housing provision and competition, particularly concerning new development.

With reference to the first of these issues, it became apparent in our interviews that many residents tended to discuss changing local housing markets alongside recent processes of population change and socio-cultural recomposition in villages. Indeed, housing was viewed by these respondents as both an important cause and an outcome of wider processes of change in the local area, and, as highlighted in the previous chapter, was capable of being utilized as an important cultural symbol with which to contest and protest against an in-movement of outside, predominantly English groups to

Table 3.3: Respondents who perceived housing change in their areas over recent times (percentages)

Teifi Valley	69.1
Devil's Bridge	64.0
Tanat Valley	48.1
Betws-y-coed	39.8
All areas	55.2

Table 3.4: Reactions to recent processes of housing change in the local area (percentages)

	Betws-y-coed	Devil's Bridge	Tanat Valley	Teifi Valley	All
Approve	40.2	17.0	43.0	39.0	34.2
No particular feelings or don't know	29.9	30.5	29.8	30.2	30.2
Disapprove	29.9	55.4	27.1	30.8	35.6

the area. Many Welsh-speaking respondents referred to the greater affluence of most English in-movers, which enabled them to outbid local groups, and particularly younger residents. Housing, then, was viewed by these residents as acting as a key route into and out of the local housing market for different groups, with such movements being perceived predominantly as detrimental to local community cohesion and culture:

> A lot more middle- and upper-class English [are] buying cheap property – cheap to them. Again [I strongly disapprove]; it's to do with the structure and ethics of society. (2067, Devil's Bridge)

> The English coming in . . . I'm not a Welsh nationalist but Welsh people should have more chance. [The] English [are] affecting the prices – selling houses in London and such and buying here. (4056, Teifi Valley)

> [More] affluent English people, especially of retirement age. [They have] escalated local prices of housing beyond the means of local people. [The] locality [is] losing its character. Local children [are] losing their first language. (4198, Teifi Valley)

Another important aspect of housing change discussed by respondents concerned the increased provision of private housing for sale in local communities, and while many residents were not against housing development *per se*, a widespread disapproval was evident of the proliferation of large-scale developments over recent years. Such developments were viewed by many residents as inducing dramatic changes to the physical structure of settlements, a process that tended generally to be viewed in less than positive terms:

> Bungalows galore [have] been built. [The] village [has] extended considerably, spoiling the area. (4128, Teifi Valley)

> For such a small village, quite a few new houses have been erected. (3028, Tanat Valley)

> There has been in the past a bit of disquiet [about new housing development] because particularly Penrhyncoch developed very quickly and grew from a very small village into a much bigger one with a much more mobile population ... (Devil's Bridge clerk)

In other villages, particularly in the Teifi Valley, ribbon development was mentioned by several respondents as an important local issue, with the distinctiveness of villages being threatened by a continuum of housing development along roads. In such responses, complaints were evident about practices of illegal planning consents which were allowing such developments to take place (this issue is also discussed later in this chapter):

> New bungalows [are] springing up, [there] doesn't seem to be any planning controls on them – erratic ribbon development with no structure to it. (4138, Teifi Valley)

> Bungalows [are] growing like mushrooms [with] infill and incursion into the countryside. They are spoiling it [the local area]. (4075, Teifi Valley)

Furthermore, the predominance of bungalows and housing estates was viewed as raising important design issues, given that, for several respondents, the architectural style of these new dwellings tended generally to be out of character with existing properties in the local area:

> Several new houses have been built. [You have to] question their appearance. What do they add to Llangynog? [It is] possible to have constructed them in a different manner to avoid the apparent eyesores. (3056, Tanat Valley)

Tatty, modern bungalows have been built with no character and wrongly coloured roofs. (2097, Devil's Bridge)

Again, some residents linked the nature of these new developments to recent processes of social and cultural change in their local areas, given that such housing schemes have tended to be characterized generally by small numbers of large dwellings, built for private sale at the higher range of the price scale (see Milbourne, 1997). Thus, amongst these residents, this executive-type development was viewed as initiating important changes in local social compositions – attracting more affluent groups into villages, and pushing out lower-income groups, particularly younger residents, from the local area in search of more affordable housing opportunities:

[There is] no local opposition to new housing as long as it meets local demand . . . People realize that if we want younger people to stay in the village we have to build . . . (Betws-y-coed clerk)

English people come here because of the prices and the houses that have been recently built. (4162, Teifi Valley)

Housing is too expensive for local people. [There is a] good case for building cheaper housing for young couples and elderly people . . . Salaries here are very low, so some will never afford to buy their own property. (3219, Teifi Valley)

In addition to the high price of properties (relative to local income levels) associated with new developments, other residents in our survey pointed to what we might call a gentrification of the existing housing stock, with groups of in-moving households purchasing and improving older, run-down (and, in some cases, derelict) properties. While this 'tidying up' of local housing was largely welcomed by many respondents, some complained about the knock-on effects of outside groups buying up relatively low-cost properties (for newcomers), particularly in terms of the escalation of local house prices beyond the means of many local people:

Prices are going up all the time, even derelict properties. (2200, Devil's Bridge)

[There] used to be a lot of derelict properties, [now they are] all doing them up. (1177, Betws-y-coed)

Other respondents though, made reference to a number of social and economic benefits associated with this gentrification of derelict dwellings with new residents able to support a range of local services, although in some of the comments that follow it is possible to detect feelings of regret about associated cultural changes and young people leaving their home villages:

> Either the English people buy the cottages and therefore keep them in good condition or they simply become derelict because there's no need for them. (1093, Betws-y-coed)

> [The] Welsh have moved away and the English have come in their place. [I'm] pleased to see some people living here instead of empty houses. [Interviewer's comment: I notice this man's sadness at the change, but in my opinion his natural reticence and politeness keeps him from commenting.] (3207, Tanat Valley)

> [There has been an] influx of southerners. If the[se] people didn't come, the properties would only lay empty. Youngsters simply can't afford the high prices. (3055, Tanat Valley)

While the rapid scale of housing development was regarded as a key issue in many villages, in other settlements, particularly those located outside designated development areas, several residents were keen to point out that, while they were aware of development in nearby settlements, there had been relatively little new housing built in their local area over recent years. Such a situation of non-growth was particularly true in one of the villages in the Betws-y-coed study area which was owned and managed by the National Trust, and also in some of the smaller villages in the Devil's Bridge area:

> There's only one house been built since I've been born (seventy-five years ago) and there is planning permission for only two other homes to be built but one has been there for twelve to fifteen years. (Betws-y-coed clerk)

> [PM: has there been any opposition towards new housing development?] No, not here, unlike similar villages within the region there hasn't been any estates of housing here, as compared with Penrhyncoch. (Devil's Bridge clerk)

Another important housing issue which has emerged in areas of the Welsh countryside over the last couple of decades has been that of holiday-home and second-home ownership. A number of studies have investigated whether such housing represents a 'curse or blessing' (Coppock, 1977), and groups such as Meibion Glyndŵr have attempted to use leisure homes as an example of the economic and cultural exploitation of local Welsh-speaking communities by English-owned capital. Across our study areas, leisure-home ownership appeared to be most prominent in Betws-y-coed – accounting for around one in five of all properties – while such homes made up between 4 and 9 per cent of the local housing stock in the other three areas. Notwithstanding such a high level of second- and holiday-home ownership in the Betws-y-coed study area, interviews with several community council clerks in other areas revealed that the impact of this particular housing issue had reduced dramatically since the 1970s, both in terms of physical numbers of leisure properties and the cultural tensions and conflicts associated with such ownership:

> There's a lot of them [second and holiday homes]. [PM: Is that a problem?] – I don't think so no, we seem to be getting so used to them now, but I'm sure there is 25 per cent of the community that is holiday homes. (Tanat Valley clerk)

> Very few [second homes] – there were quite a number here, but the numbers have dropped. Many have been sold – ten years ago second homes were a problem ... but you can't call it a problem now. (Teifi Valley clerk)

> There are a few [second homes]. At one time that used to raise its ugly head all the time. It's quietened down now – a lot of people can't afford them any more. (Teifi Valley clerk)

Access to local housing markets

In the introduction to this chapter attention was given to some key tenurial changes which have taken place in Welsh rural housing markets over recent years, linked particularly to the increased dominance of the private sector as housing provider. Similar patterns of changing housing provision were also evident in our four study

Table 3.5: Household tenure

	Owned outright	Owned on mortgage	Social rented	Private rented	Other
Betws-y-coed	71.5	10.8	10.0	6.0	1.6
Devil's Bridge	44.8	34.1	8.1	11.7	1.3
Tanat Valley	44.2	20.2	12.8	16.9	5.8
Teifi Valley	43.6	23.7	19.5	9.8	3.6
All areas	51.2	21.9	12.7	11.0	3.0

areas. Overall local housing markets were dominated by the private sector in terms of both new and existing properties, and accounted for the tenure of 84.1 per cent of all households across these areas (table 3.5). Within the private sector, though, it is owner-occupation that dominates household tenure, with half of all households owning property outright and a further 22 per cent through mortgages. It is evident in this table that the level of outright ownership is considerably higher in the Betws-y-coed area, which is linked to the larger proportion of elderly residents living in this locality. Table 3.5 also highlights the impact of recent housing legislation on these local markets, particularly in relation to the low levels of social rental provision. In fact, only 11.2 per cent of households were living in council properties, and 1.5 per cent (fifteen households) were renting from housing associations. Moreover, even with such a low proportion of households in the rented sector, our survey findings would seem to suggest an uneven distribution of rental opportunities between the study areas, with social rental accommodation accounting for 8.1 per cent of households in the Devil's Bridge area, but 19.5 per cent of Teifi Valley households, and with private rental properties accounting for 16.9 per cent of the local housing stock in the Tanat Valley (associated predominantly with the agricultural industry) compared with only 6.0 per cent of properties in the Devil's Bridge area. It can also be suggested that such differential rental housing opportunities are evident within our study areas, with social rental accommodation, for example, tending generally to be concentrated in the larger settlements (see Milbourne, forthcoming).

In a number of commentaries highlighted earlier in the chapter, attention was focused on the strong purchasing power associated with many newcomer households in local areas, and the effects of such buying power on the housing opportunities available to younger local residents. The Lifestyles research would appear to point to factors within and outside local housing markets as important in this respect. In relation to housing factors, property-price data collected from both our Welsh and English Lifestyles projects would seem to indicate that each of our Welsh study areas is characterized by relatively low house prices. In fact, 63.8 per cent of owner-occupier respondents estimated their property to be worth less than £45,000 – only one study area in the English Lifestyles research recorded a higher proportion of such 'low-priced' properties.[1, 2] However, even though our study areas can be viewed as being dominated by low-priced property markets, it should not be assumed that local housing is affordable to all groups. For example, four out of ten households in the rural Wales surveys earned less than £10,000 per annum, compared with an average of 23.0 per cent in rural England[3] (see chapter 5 for a more detailed discussion of income levels in these four study areas).

This combination of increased competition for housing, rising property prices, executive-type development, a reduction in social rental accommodation, and a low-wage economy can be seen to have led to a mismatch between housing demand and supply, and situations of housing need in many parts of rural Wales. Clearly, the extreme instance of housing need concerns those households who lack a home – the homeless; and while the household-based nature of our survey inevitably excluded any exploration of this particular housing problem, it remains the case that levels of homelessness have increased at a faster rate in rural Wales than in Wales as a whole over the late 1980s and early 1990s (see Welsh Office, 1986b, 1992). Our interviews, though, did discuss with residents in households and key local actors, some general issues concerning housing problems and need within their areas. Table 3.6, for example, shows that slightly more than half of our respondents considered that there were groups in the local area who were experiencing housing problems, although the recognition of housing need varied considerably between our study areas (perceptions of such problems were greatest in the Devil's Bridge and Tanat Valley areas – mentioned by 70.0 and 69.0 per cent of respondents respectively).

Both residents and community clerks identified younger members of local communities as the group experiencing the greatest difficulties in finding suitable housing. In fact, our survey of residents indicated that 31.2 per cent of those recognizing local housing

Table 3.6: Perceptions that local people are experiencing difficulties in finding accommodation (percentages)

Devil's Bridge	70.0
Tanat Valley	69.0
Teifi Valley	48.4
Betws-y-coed	42.8
All areas	57.0

need referred to the plight of young married couples, 26.5 per cent mentioned young single people and a further 13.4 per cent of respondents brought up problems faced by school leavers:

I believe young people possibly [are experiencing housing difficulties] – young people getting married or not getting married and living together. (Teifi Valley clerk)

There is a common problem throughout the country. Young people find it difficult to afford a house in their area. (Devil's Bridge clerk)

Clearly, these perceptions of housing problems faced by younger members of these local communities would appear to reinforce key findings from a number of other studies concerning housing need in rural Wales and beyond (see, for example, Association of County Councils, 1989; Community Action for Social and Economic Development, 1989).

Rather surprisingly, though, other key groups commonly associated with sets of housing problems in rural areas were less frequently mentioned by our respondents – the unemployed were mentioned by 8.0 per cent of residents in our surveys, and only 2.6 per cent pointed to problems faced by the elderly. Such low levels of perception, however, may be explained, in the former case, by the popular image of low levels of unemployment in rural Wales and the fact that the unemployed are entitled to housing benefit; and in the latter, this seems to reflect a feeling that elderly groups are relatively well catered for within existing rural housing markets.

In general terms, the main perceived housing problem faced by young people across our four study areas – mentioned by around two-thirds of all respondents – related to a shortage of affordable accommodation for both purchase and rental (see table 3.7). Interestingly, most residents felt that it was supply-side factors that were most important in this respect, with relatively few people

Table 3.7: Main problems facing young people seeking accommodation (percentages)

	Betws-y-coed	Devil's Bridge	Tanat Valley	Teifi Valley	All
No problems	19.2	3.6	8.5	10.5	9.9
Shortage of affordable housing for purchase	41.4	35.1	46.1	34.5	38.9
Shortage of affordable housing for rent	9.8	20.0	12.2	20.9	16.1
Shortage of council housing	6.5	15.3	6.8	15.9	11.5
Competition from affluent migrants	14.7	6.9	11.9	3.0	9.0
Difficulty in obtaining mortgages	3.9	12.4	2.4	4.1	6.3
Other	4.6	6.7	12.2	11.1	8.4

pointing to the effects of competition from more affluent migrants on housing opportunities available to younger residents:

It is mentioned from time to time that the difficulty, which is pretty general throughout Wales I would imagine, the difficulty for young people to have starter homes – there's very little provision for that. (Devil's Bridge clerk)

I'm sure it [more council housing] would be very welcome by a lot of these people. It would be an answer to the question for many people, as a start as it were. (Devil's Bridge clerk)

[There is a] need for increased council provision. We have houses built especially for the older people by Tai Teifi, but we need a lot more houses for younger people to rent. (Teifi Valley clerk)

Table 3.7 also identifies some important variations in the perception of housing need across our study areas, with a shortage of reasonably priced housing for purchase representing more of an issue in Betws-y-coed and the Tanat Valley than in the other two areas, where a lack of affordable rental opportunities was considered of similar importance to private market provision.

While most residents in our surveys recognized sets of housing problems, and particularly problems affecting younger residents, the causes of such problems were seen as located predominantly outside the realm of housing. Housing changes and problems were viewed frequently as outcomes of more general economic factors, particularly low-wage economies, with many young people tending to leave rural areas altogether, or else move to nearby towns, in order to secure higher-quality, better-paid employment opportunities:

> I know of no specific examples [of people moving out through a lack of affordable housing] but I know that it is a problem for young people and I dare say there are some people living in rented accommodation in Aberystwyth that would be much happier living out in the country were that feasible. But as for leaving and packing their bags altogether and leaving the area, I don't know of any specific examples, apart from what generally happens through [a lack of] employment opportunities. (Devil's Bridge clerk)

> [Housing is] not one of the main factors behind people moving out. People are moving out for more employment-based reasons – that's a very important factor. (Betws-y-coed clerk)

> [For] young people, there's no housing need as such because of [the type of] work we've got to offer – there's nothing like that. They move to Aberystwyth or wherever. (Devil's Bridge clerk)

Housing tensions and conflicts

Our interviews with local residents also explored the extent and nature of a range of housing-based tensions and conflicts in each area. Again, the interlinkages between restructuring of the housing market and socio-cultural recomposition were discussed frequently by those respondents mentioning localized housing tensions. Here, residents pointed frequently to the increased buying power of newcomer groups and rising property prices, particularly associated with new developments, as acting to alter existing social structures and reduce feelings of cultural distinctiveness and community in many villages:

> There are difficulties with English buyers pricing Welsh buyers out of the market ... Feelings are very high and it is becoming difficult for young people to buy houses. (2093, Devil's Bridge)

> English people can afford to buy the houses and the Welsh want to keep the village Welsh-speaking. (1208, Betws-y-coed)

[Any bad feelings over housing?] Not for myself, but I think that some of the older Welsh people are resentful of the English people. They come here and they don't really mix in the community. It used to be a very Welsh-speaking community. (2163, Devil's Bridge)

The situation of younger residents in securing accommodation was also mentioned by residents in terms of the changing provision of housing in local areas. The nature of new provision, together with a dramatic reduction in social rental opportunities was seen by many respondents as creating a set of housing-based tensions in their local area:

Council house lists [are] long [and] low-income people find it difficult to find houses. (2116, Devil's Bridge)

Young local people tend to get quite irate at the difficulty in obtaining rented accommodation. (4198, Teifi Valley)

People [are] having to move out of the area because [of] no suitable accommodation. (1056, Betws-y-coed)

A range of tensions concerning the allocation of social and private rental housing was also revealed in these interviews. In some situations, the rehousing of officially recognized groups in need was viewed by certain respondents as conflicting with their understandings of local housing need, and individual households were accused of 'jumping the queue' for council housing. More generally, though, a number of influential actors were seen as holding the key (often, quite literally) to rental accommodation opportunities in the local area. In the case of social rental housing, and particularly council properties, the influence of a small number of local councillors was seen, by certain residents, as crucial to securing such accommodation:

Local people on [the] council waiting list get upset by someone coming in from Merthyr [a town located around forty miles away] rather than a local person getting a house that comes free. (4065, Teifi Valley)

It's who you know around here isn't it? Some of them are getting council houses – they know the councillors, that sort of thing. (2163, Devil's Bridge)

Council members seem to have their own code of preference. [I] can't really grumble as it's [a] 'who you know and not what you know' way of the world. (3057, Tanat Valley)

The councillors certainly seem to know which strings to pull. [It's] a case of favouritism. (3054, Tanat Valley)

In other areas, though, residents mentioned different key actors who were influential within rental markets. In one village in the Tanat Valley, the Severn Trent water company was seen as an important landlord, while in another village in the Betws-y-coed area, several residents complained about the way the Forestry Commission was selling off its rented housing stock at prices beyond the reach of many local people:

People who know Severn Trent members get priority when it comes to waiting for houses. (3125, Tanat Valley)

[The] Forestry Commission is selling houses in the area. Local people couldn't afford the prices they were asking for them. (1222, Betws-y-coed)

The influence of a few local actors in being able to 'work the system' was seen as not only linked to rental housing allocation but also to the development of new housing schemes and the planning decision-making process. Indeed, a recent report from the Welsh Affairs Committee on affordable housing in rural areas has highlighted a number of cases where planning permissions for certain dwellings have been granted outside designated areas (House of Commons, 1992/3; See also Cloke, 1996, for a comprehensive review of the committee's findings in relation to this particular point). One resident in our survey, for example, when asked whether there were any individuals or organizations who were influential in the local housing market, responded:

Local planning officers and people who know them, or who are related to them – the 'Tafia'. (2067, Devil's Bridge)

while another person commented that, in terms of planning permission,

Some get it, some don't! (4146, Tanat Valley).

Finally, in terms of housing-based tensions, the influence of some of these local actors was viewed by several, mainly English, newcomer respondents as acting to discriminate against other residents in their study area who, for a number of reasons, remained external to these local networks of power:

> The English feel discriminated against by the Welsh – people have got cross. (2054, Devil's Bridge)

> People get fed up with the Welsh housing association – [it] builds houses only for Welsh-speakers. (4123, Teifi Valley)

Housing conditions

Research on rural housing, over the last twenty or so years, has tended to be concerned more with issues of competition and need than the physical conditions of housing in the countryside. Indeed, with the wide-scale improvements made to the rural housing stock in the post-war period, it is commonly assumed that poor housing conditions no longer constitute a significant problem. However, while such a statement may hold true for the vast majority of rural dwellings, Rogers (1987) has pointed to increases in the number of sub-standard properties in the English countryside over recent years, particularly amongst lower-income households. Indeed, it can be suggested that, with the dramatic reduction of social rental properties over the 1980s and early 1990s, the issue of housing disrepair, particularly in the private rented sector may become more important over the next few years.

In the case of rural Wales, statistics from a recent housing-conditions survey (Welsh Office, 1986a) point to several rural districts which contain much higher proportions of sub-standard properties than are found in urban areas of Wales. For example, while a similar proportion of properties in rural[4] and urban areas were classified by the 1986 survey as 'unfit' (7.6 per cent compared to a Welsh average of 7.2 per cent), the rural district of Dwyfor reported the highest incidence of unfitness in Wales at 16.9 per cent, and the districts of Ceredigion, Dinefwr and Preseli each recorded rates of unfitness in excess of 10 per cent of all dwellings.

Our survey of households has highlighted, as might be expected, some key variations in the conditions of housing stock within and between our study areas, reflecting a whole host of historical and contemporary factors, including recent developments in high-quality and -priced developments in larger settlements, design restrictions imposed on housing in certain areas of countryside (for example, in the Snowdonia National Park), the legacy of the mining industry in parts of the Devil's Bridge and Betws-y-coed areas, and the gentrification of stock initiated by more affluent in-movers and holiday-home companies. In terms of some key inter-area variations in housing size and types, the Betws-y-coed area recorded the lowest percentage of houses with one living room (14.9 per cent), the Tanat Valley the highest at 53.3 per cent of all properties. The Betws-y-coed study area also contained the greatest proportion of dwellings containing three living rooms (21.4 per cent), while the Teifi Valley recorded the lowest level at 5.8 per cent. A similar picture of housing types emerges in terms of the number of bedrooms, with the Betws-y-coed, Devil's Bridge and Teifi Valley area recording at least double the number of four-bedroom properties found in the Tanat Valley.

Our survey also revealed the existence of considerable variations in the availability of specific household amenities. One pertinent example of such amenities is the number of households with and without central heating; table 3.8 highlights the Teifi Valley as recording the highest proportion of dwellings with such heating (86.3 per cent) and the Tanat Valley the least at 69.3 per cent. Nevertheless, in overall terms around three-quarters of properties in the survey contained some kind of central heating.

With regard to other household amenities, all dwellings in the Betws-y-coed area and over 95 per cent of houses in the other three areas had mains electricity, but less than 3 per cent of dwellings in the Tanat Valley, Teifi Valley and Devil's Bridge areas were connected to a mains gas supply (table 3.9). Significantly, though, the study areas varied in terms of their connection to a mains drainage system. Under one-quarter of houses in the Betws-y-coed, Teifi Valley and Tanat Valley areas relied on a septic tank, compared with 60 per cent of houses in the Devil's Bridge area.

Although our survey did not prompt respondents on this particular point, these variations in the levels of some infrastructural services may have important repercussions in the future. With such services now being supplied by private-sector companies, fears have been

Table 3.8: Households with central heating (percentages)

Teifi Valley	86.3
Devil's Bridge	73.8
Betws-y-coed	72.4
Tanat Valley	69.3
All areas	75.6

Table 3.9: The presence of essential amenities within households (percentages)

	Betws-y-coed	Devil's Bridge	Tanat Valley	Teifi Valley	All
Mains electricity	100.0	98.2	96.8	99.2	98.6
Mains gas	32.0	0.9	2.4	2.0	9.3
Mains water	96.8	83.6	89.2	96.1	91.4
Mains drainage	90.8	40.5	78.0	85.3	73.7
Sole use of flush WC	98.0	96.9	97.9	98.8	97.9
Sink and cold water tap	99.6	99.1	98.3	98.8	99.0
Running hot water	98.0	95.5	97.0	98.4	97.4
Fixed bath/shower	96.8	95.9	96.6	98.4	97.0
Gas/electric cooker	98.4	98.6	96.6	97.7	97.8

expressed that once initial safeguards on charges are relaxed the differential cost of supplying services will be passed on directly to the consumer (see Bell and Cloke, 1989). We believe that this could mean that rural residents will pay substantially more for connection to, and upkeep of, infrastructural services, given the higher cost of providing those services to a low-density and scattered network of dwellings. Occasional comments from respondents suggested some support for this belief, although it remained a largely unvoiced concern of rural residents.

Otherwise our surveys revealed that the level of facilities in dwellings was consistent with an acceptable standard of living in all but a few cases. The vast majority of households had sole use of a running hot-water supply, a fixed indoor bath or shower, a gas or electric cooker, and an indoor flush WC (table 3.9). There were still, however, just a few exceptions to this standardization, including six households in the Devil's Bridge area, three in the Tanat Valley, and two in the Betws-y-coed area which did not have an indoor toilet. In another case, one of our interview team recorded the following housing situation, which would appear to suggest the

Table 3.10: Households with structural defects (percentages)

Devil's Bridge	19.6
Tanat Valley	12.1
Teifi Valley	12.0
Betws-y-coed	6.8
All areas	12.4

continuation of inadequate housing conditions (normatively defined) in areas of the Welsh countryside:

> Two brothers lived here and had done so for between forty and sixty years ... Their house was extremely spartan and smelt strange. I came out of there with fleas on me ... They only had a small cooker, a huge open fire with half a tree in it (in the middle of summer), a table and a few chairs, no bathroom and no bath. They said they used the river [to wash]. I asked them how often and they thought it a funny question. (2168, Devil's Bridge)

While the vast majority of respondents expressed a general satisfaction with the physical condition of their property, our survey also revealed a significant minority of mainly elderly households living in sub-standard (according to respondents) dwellings. Table 3.10 shows that around one in five respondents in the Devil's Bridge area, and 12 per cent in the Tanat Valley and Teifi Valley areas reported a range of structural defects associated with their properties, and these were much higher than those recorded in the Lifestyles in Rural England research (where, only 7.7 per cent reported such defects). Four broad types of defect appeared important – accounting for around three-quarters of those reported: problems of dampness (35.1 per cent); leaking roofs (14.9 per cent); loose brickwork and plasterwork (14.9 per cent); and problems with windows and doors (11.3 per cent). Although many of these defects were viewed by respondents as relatively minor problems, slightly more than one-third considered that they constituted a danger to the health of persons in the household – a level almost double that reported for the English Rural Lifestyles study.

Conclusion

In this chapter we have stressed the importance of considering the interconnections between the material and symbolic roles played by housing in the Welsh countryside – roles which are linked to issues of housing change, problems and conflicts. It is clear that some residents in our study areas tended to discuss recent processes of housing change in wider socio-cultural terms; as facilitating an in-flow of more affluent outside (usually English) groups, and also bringing about a forced displacement of many low-income, younger Welsh-speaking residents from their villages. As such, for these respondents at least, local housing issues in their villages were capable of being understood only in relation to the types of cultural changes and conflicts discussed in the previous chapter.

Alongside housing problems and conflicts associated with social and cultural issues, though, frequent reference was made by many residents in our survey to the changing provision and allocation of housing in rural Wales. While previous policy issues of the physical condition of the rural housing stock and provision of key amenities would appear to represent less pressing concerns in the 1990s Welsh countryside, a large proportion of local authority officials, community council clerks and respondents expressed considerable concern about the quality of life of groups of households within and outside housing markets in rural Wales. Such concern was linked predominantly to changing central-government housing policies over the 1980s and early 1990s, and the increasing domination of the private sector as both housing supplier and allocator. Indeed, the lack of affordability of much of the owner-occupied dwellings in the private housing sector, and the shrinkage of social rented housing opportunities were perceived by many respondents in our survey as constituting a key threat to the continued survival of villages as places of mixed-age and socio-cultural groupings. Obviously, detailed local needs surveys would have to be carried out in a comprehensive manner before specific levels of need could be established in any given area, but the qualitative information from our surveys strongly suggested that respondents were deeply concerned about the future for those of their young people who wished to remain in the area. Indeed, in some of the commentaries presented in this chapter, it has been possible to sense from our respondents feelings of despair and hopelessness about the 'inevitability' of losing local young people from the villages of rural Wales unless policies are introduced on a wider and more compre-hensive scale to provide affordable housing in these places.

Notes

[1] It should be noted that property prices were rising at the time of inter-viewing and that many owner-occupiers may have been basing their estimates of the price of their housing on historical benchmarks, although such a suggestion would also apply to the English research.

[2] The English research – Lifestyles in Rural England – involved a survey of 3,000 households in twelve study areas and was published by the Rural Development Commission in 1993.

[3] The twelve study areas in Lifestyles in Rural England.

[4] Those districts defined as extreme rural by Cloke and Edwards (1986)

References

Association of County Councils (1989) *Homes We Can Afford*, Association of County Councils, London.

Bell, P. and Cloke, P. (1989) 'The changing relationship between the private and the public sectors: privatisation in rural Britain', *Journal of Rural Studies*, 5, 1–16.

Bollom, C. (1978) *Attitudes and Second Homes in Rural Wales*, University of Wales Press, Cardiff.

Cloke, P. (1996) 'Housing in the open countryside: windows on "irresponsible" planning in rural Wales', *Town Planning Review*, 67 (3), 291–308.

Cloke, P. and Edwards, G (1986) 'Rurality in England and Wales 1981', *Regional Studies*, 20, 289–306.

Community Action for Social and Economic Development (1989) *Rural Wales*, CASED.

Coppock, J. (1977) *Second Homes: Curse or Blessing?* Pergamon Press, Oxford.

House of Commons (1992/3) Welsh Affairs Committee, Third Report, *Rural Housing 2*, HMSO, London.

Jones, N. (1993) *Living in Rural Wales*, Gomer Press, Llandysul.

Milbourne, P. (1993) *The Dynamics of the Housing Market in Rural Wales*, unpublished Ph.D. thesis, University of Wales, Aberystwyth.

Milbourne, P. (1997) 'Housing conflict and domestic property classes in rural Wales', *Environment and Planning A*, vol. 29, pp.43–62.

Milbourne, P. (forthcoming) 'Social housing in rural areas: changing patterns of provision and allocation'.

Office of Population and Census Surveys (1992) *1991 Census of Population*, OPCS, London.

Rogers, A. (1987) 'Issues in English rural housing: an assessment and prospect', in D. MacGregor, D. Robertson and M. Shucksmith (eds.), *Rural Housing in Scotland: Recent Research and Policy*, Aberdeen University Press, Aberdeen.

Tai Cymru (1990a) *Housing Aspirations of Young People in Rural Wales*, Tai Cymru, Cardiff.

Tai Cymru (1990b) *The Demand for Social Housing in Rural Wales*, Tai Cymru, Cardiff.

Welsh Office (1986a) *The Welsh House Condition Survey 1986*, Welsh Office, Cardiff.

Welsh Office (1986b) *Welsh Housing Statistics*, Welsh Office, Cardiff.

Welsh Office (1989) *Land for Low Cost Housing in Rural Areas of Wales*, Draft PPG, Welsh Office, Cardiff.

Welsh Office (1992) *Welsh Housing Statistics*, Welsh Office, Cardiff.

4 • The Rural Economy and Rural Employment

Introduction

The changing nature of lifestyles in rural Wales is closely connected to the changing economy. Indeed, the issues of social, cultural, demographic and housing change which we have already discussed are at least in part bound up with the changing nature of employment. As Champion and Watkins point out,

> recent trends in population (in rural Britain) have been closely paralleled by overall patterns of employment change. (1991, 9)

These broad patterns of change have been widely recognized by rural commentators (see, for example, Archbishop's Commission on Rural Areas, 1990; Blunden and Curry, 1988; Gilg, 1991; Robinson, 1990). Whereas agriculture accounted for some 40 per cent of employment in Britain in 1800, by the 1980s it had fallen to around 2 per cent – a lower level than any other member state of the European Community. Although such aggregate figures obscure local variations, and agricultural employment accounted for 15 per cent of the *rural* workforce during the 1980s, it is still the case that farming-related jobs have continuously declined in their importance to local labour markets. Thus, although rural areas depend for their rurality at least in part on the *landscapes* of agriculture, the rural economy depends less and less on farming work. This has obvious policy implications which we will discuss further later in the chapter.

Researchers on rural employment have tended to place considerable emphasis on the increases in rural manufacturing jobs throughout the 1980s (Fothergill and Gudgin, 1982; Keeble, 1984). This interest in rural manufacturing was partly generated by a desire to examine the so-called 'urban–rural shift', and was thus promoted by those more interested in the de-industrialization being experienced in Britain's urban areas. In a desire to draw a contrast with rapid employment loss in urban areas, the impacts of manufacturing growth in rural areas were often overstated. It should be remembered that although rural manufacturing employment increased by 20 per cent between 1960 and 1987, this increase represents only some 100,000 jobs in total. It is also the case that the definitions of 'rural' adopted by some researchers of urban-to-rural manufacturing 'shifts' include some very sizeable urban settlements (see Hodge and Monk, 1987; Thrift, 1987; Cloke, 1987). There has also been considerable regional variation in manufacturing growth, and certainly in the remoter rural regions such as north and west Wales, most of the recent increases in rural employment have come in the service sector, and here the importance of small businesses and self-employment should not be underestimated. Despite this importance, which is confirmed by the results of our survey, less academic work has been done on the rural service sector. However, we can discern five important trends which underlie these broader changes.

Continued industrialization

Some limited rural areas have proved attractive to high-tech or other industrial plants, especially those areas close to motorway corridors and where greenfield sites are readily available. Here there appears to be a balance struck between the wish to achieve savings in land and rent costs, and the wish to live and work in a cherished rural environment. State agencies have been active in providing various forms of subsidy to attract investment into rural areas which are outside those zones currently favoured by market trends. In England the Rural Development Commission has nominated twenty-seven Rural Development Areas (RDAs) and two Coalfield Priority Areas in which special action has been taken to make geographically or economically peripheral areas more attractive to employers. A recent report (PA Cambridge Economic Consultants, 1992) on *Business Success in the Countryside* suggested that a good part of the new enterprise that had developed in rural areas had stemmed from migrants who were attracted to rural areas because of a perceived quality of life.

Boom-bust in resource industries

The decline of agriculture has already been mentioned, but agricultural diversification may yet bring about a mini-boom in employment associated with new farm enterprises. Other resource-based industries have also witnessed cyclical trends, for example the sequence of boom–bust–boom in rural areas around Aberdeen because of the ups and downs of the North Sea oil industry. The initial explorations now occurring in the northern sectors of Cardigan Bay may yet bring this type of boom–bust industry to rural Wales.

Service-sector growth

Growth in the service sector has taken many forms. During the 1960s and 1970s there was substantial public-sector growth as local authorities, health, education and utility services brought a spread of service jobs into rural areas. There has also been an initial introduction of technology-led service jobs, as the new information technologies have been brought into traditionally less accessible places, thereby offering connections to the urban-based service economy. On a small scale, the growth of homeworking or telecottaging in this context is likely to be lifestyle-led. On a larger scale, on-line work processing (for example, wage, credit-card-transaction, insurance-claim and air-ticket administration) will come to rural areas in search of inexpensive labour forces (and low office-rent costs). Such enterprises will be prone to similar boom–bust cycles to those that hit rural manufacturing some twenty years previously, and do not therefore seem in a position to act as long-term saviours of the rural economy as some are beginning to claim. Information technology and electronic communication may well be able to overcome the problems of distance and isolation which rural areas have suffered from, but this in itself simply allows these places to compete in a global labour market. It does not guarantee employment. Indeed, broadly there seem to be distinct similarities between these 'branch-line' service enterprises and the manufacturing branch-plants, which were the first to be closed when recession began. Growth in service jobs has also occurred in the financial services sector (e.g. estate agents, banks, solicitors) and in the construction trades (e.g. building, decorating, plumbing, electrical contracting) – all of these have been particularly sensitive to the financial squeeze and relatively slow housing markets of the late 1980s and early 1990s.

Commodification

Service-sector jobs have also arisen as rural environments have proved attractive for the demands of contemporary consumption.

Such jobs have been generated partly by new forms of recreation, leisure and tourism, which have been able to encourage visitors into a more privatized 'pay-as-you-enter' countryside. They have also been generated in response to the development of particular styles of living, through special niches in the housing market, such as retirement/sunshine/twilight communities.

Exploiting rural marginality

Some enterprises are attracted to rural locations through the expedient siting of dangerous, polluting or otherwise politically sensitive operations. Here they find not only an 'out-of-sight, out-of-mind' location, but often a grateful and potentially dependent workforce. Such enterprises include nuclear installations, the dumping of wastes of all types and levels, the treatment of industrial residues, military training facilities (a traditional rural land use), prisons and the like. Although rural areas cannot be treated as a whole in this context, there are fears that some rural places could end up as repositories for otherwise socially unacceptable, and generally unwanted, processes, as is already the case in parts of the USA (see Sandefur, 1988).

It is relatively easy to identify and chart these underlying trends in the rural economy. It is altogether more difficult to seek theoretical explanations for their current shape. This is due partly to their complexity, and partly to the difficulty of 'importing' urban-based frameworks of economic change into a rural context. Concepts and ideas which have dominated recent debates in economic geography, such as de-industrialization, the transition from Fordism to post-Fordism, new industrial spaces and flexible accumulation, are difficult to apply to the rural economy. Since the decline of agriculture, the economy of the countryside has become highly differentiated, and rural researchers have been struggling to come to terms with an increasingly complex economic situation. In the context of the large increases in rural manufacturing employment in the 1970s, research increasingly turned to a political-economy approach which stressed capital accumulation and capital restructuring (see Cloke, 1989, for a review). In this analysis rural areas were conceptually linked to their urban counterparts as arenas of investment for successive waves of footloose capital. However, this itself now seems inadequate in the light of rural labour markets which are dominated by the service sector. In the

Aberystwyth and Conwy and Colwyn travel-to-work areas, which contain Devil's Bridge and Betws-y-coed respectively, 82 per cent of all employment is in the service sector (Welsh Economic Trends, 1996, 103–7). These are amongst the highest percentages of any travel-to-work area in the country. However, even models of service-sector change are difficult to apply to the very specialized circumstances of these particular local economies. The service-sector here, as opposed to many urban areas with high service-sector employment, is not dominated by routine clerical office work. Instead, it is a mixture of retail, tourism, self-employment, and public- and private-sector services. It remains a key task for rural researchers to conceptualize these changes. The productionist definition of the rural economy based on a sectoral analysis of agriculture is clearly outdated, but it is not sufficient merely to inport urban-based models of service-sector development. We need to develop theories which are sensitive to the particular and increasingly differentiated trajectories of rural employment.

The contemporary economy of rural Wales

These trends of course manifest themselves differently in different places, and they combine in different ways, and with a range of other processes, to produce distinctive local patterns of employment. Before we discuss our four study areas in detail, we will set the context by considering the economy of rural Wales as a whole. Table 4.1 and Figure 4.1 give the broad structure of employment in the DBRW area. They confirm the continuing long-term decline of agriculture, which now employs less than 10 per cent of the rural workforce. Services are by far the dominant sector of employment, accounting for 69 per cent of jobs. Construction employs 4 per cent of the workforce, whilst the remaining 18 per cent work in production industries, including energy supply and mineral extraction. Manufacturing alone provides 14 per cent of employment within the Objective 5b area (Blackaby et al., 1995, 274). This figure however marks wide regional disparities – manufacturing accounts for 24 per cent of all jobs in the former district of Montgomeryshire but only 8 per cent in Ceredigion.

There are also wide variations in levels of unemployment throughout the area. As the recent White Paper for Rural Wales

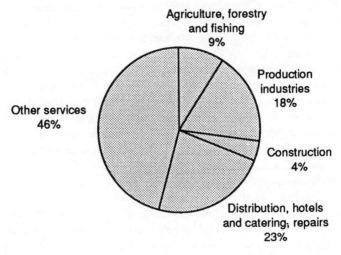

Figure 4.1: Employee structure in DBRW area, 1991.
Source: Census of Employment.

Table 4.1: Employee structure in DBRW area

Standard Industrial Classification	1989 Number	1989 Per cent	1991 Number	1991 Per cent	Wales 1991 (per cent)
Agriculture, forestry and fishing	7036	9.9	6528	9.5	2.2
Energy and water supply industries	2343	3.3	1921	2.8	2.5
Extraction of minerals and ores other than fuels; manufacture of metals, mineral products and chemicals	1227	1.7	1133	1.6	4.9
Metal goods, engineering and vehicle industries	4155	5.8	4021	5.8	9.4
Other manufacturing industries	6820	9.5	5536	8.0	8.5
Construction	2024	2.8	2519	3.7	4.8
Distribution, hotels and catering; repairs	15564	21.8	16096	23.4	20.8
Transport and communication	2621	3.7	2404	3.5	4.8
Banking, finance insurance, business services and leasing	3894	5.5	3714	5.4	7.4
Other services (a)	25638	35.9	24971	36.3	34.8
Total	71322	100.0	68843	100.0	100.0

(a) Includes 'unclassified by industry'
Source: Census of Employment.

points out, parts of rural Wales 'have an enviable record of employment' (Welsh Office, 1996, 44). These however tend to be the parts which are within commuting distance of the more successful larger towns, where underemployment in agriculture and seasonal unemployment in tourism are masked by high rates of service-sector employment in the towns themselves. The most successful travel-to-work areas (TTWAs) in terms of employment confirm this – Newtown, Welshpool, Carmarthen, Llandeilo, Brecon, Denbigh, Llandrindod Wells and Aberystwyth were all ranked among the hundred TTWAs in the UK with the lowest unemployment (out of 334). These TTWAs are large administrative units however, and the rates for single areas, especially those centred on vibrant towns, can mask pockets of high localized unemployment in the surrounding rural areas. Indeed, those areas not centred on such towns are at the opposite end of the unemployment spectrum. The remoter rural TTWAs of Holyhead, Bangor and Caernarfon in the north, and Haverfordwest and South Pembrokeshire in the south all fall within the 100 TTWAs with the highest unemployment in the UK.

There are other discernible trends in the economy of rural Wales. Self-employment is much more important than in Wales as a whole. In the Objective 5b area, 25 per cent of the male population of working age are self-employed, compared with 13 per cent in Wales as a whole. The 8 per cent of females who are self-employed also represent twice the Welsh average. Such high levels of self-employment make the rural economy especially vulnerable, and often represent considerable underemployment for the individuals concerned. The rural economy is also made vulnerable by the predominance of small businesses. Of all businesses in rural Wales, 55 per cent employ less than four people, and less than 0.5 per cent of employers in any sector employ more than 100 (Blackaby et al., 1995, 274).

In order to assess the level of economic activity in a given area, economists use the notion of Gross Domestic Product (GDP) which calculates the value of all goods and services produced within that area. On this measure, the welfare of the rural economy is not at all encouraging. The value of GDP per head in Dyfed and Powys (calculated together for this indicator) in 1991 was only 75.5 per cent of the UK average. In Gwynedd GDP per head was 76.4 per cent of the UK average. Both figures are considerably below the value for Wales as a whole, which itself was only 85 per cent of the national average in 1991, and both had fallen in percentage terms since 1987 (ibid., 219). GDP per head was 17 per cent below the EU average in Wales in 1991, but 19 per cent lower in the rural areas (European Commission, 1995, 287). Thus, although there are undoubtedly pockets of prosperity in rural Wales, the rural economy as a whole is weak when compared with the rest of Wales, and even weaker when compared with the UK.

These general trends were all confirmed by our survey research. In each of our study areas, non-agricultural employment dominated the local economy, but since we surveyed exclusively rural areas and deliberately avoided towns, the rate of agricultural employment was inevitably higher than that for rural Wales as a whole. In three of the areas, 'agriculture, forestry and fishing' comprised less than one-fifth of the resident adult workforce. In the Tanat Valley, however, farming-related employment remained important – accounting for one-third of the total workforce. Each local labour market, to varying degrees, was dominated by the service sector, with about two-thirds of workers in the Betws-y-coed and Devil's Bridge areas, and roughly half of all persons in employment in the Tanat and Teifi Valley study areas engaged in this sector. Manufacturing was particularly under-represented in the study areas – ranging from 4.4 per cent of workers in Betws-y-coed to 11.9 per cent in the Teifi Valley, considerably less than the average for rural Wales. In spite of the reasonably high rates of agricultural employment in these four areas of rural Wales, the economy is thus heavily dependent on the service sector – both public and private.

The changing nature of the rural labour market is further illustrated by the level of those engaged in professional and managerial occupations. Professional and managerial-type employment appeared most dominant in the Devil's Bridge and Teifi Valley areas (accounting for over one-third of all employment in both areas). Such high levels presumably result from the presence of universities in Aberystwyth and Lampeter. The Tanat Valley, with 27 per cent of workers engaged in professional and managerial occupations is characterized by high levels of commuting – particularly to Oswestry, Shrewsbury and Welshpool. Betws-y-coed had the lowest levels of professional and managerial workers, but these still accounted for over 20 per cent of those in work. Here we should stress the potentially confusing nature of service-sector employment growth in rural areas. Many managers and professionals work in the urban-based service-sector, and thus the location and nature of this employment, and the associated services, have very different impacts in rural communities from other 'service-sector' work, which may very well be seasonal, low-paid and/or part-time. For example, the difference between a financial services manager and a part-time cleaner in a caravan park is enormous in work (and income and status) terms, yet both may be included in the ubiquitous category of the 'service sector'.

Although it was pointed out earlier that our survey should be viewed more as a snapshot of rural lifestyles in 1991 than as a study of changing lifestyles, we were able to cross-tabulate household occupational structures with length of residence. Persons in employment were subdivided into two groups: the first included people who had moved to their present place of residence in the previous five years; the second consisted of persons who had resided in their property for a period in excess of five years. Although it is recognized that such a categorization is rather simplistic, it nevertheless provides an indication of the occupational structure of new residents within the study areas. In general terms, our survey revealed that newcomer groups were over-represented in professional and managerial occupations (35.3 per cent, as opposed to 25.5 per cent of workers who had lived in their current property for more than five years), and under-represented in farming and related occupations (4.5 per cent/19.0 per cent). Thus, it would appear that 'newcomers' in employment are taking a much higher proportion of professional and managerial jobs – which are generally character-ized by increased stability of employment and higher levels of salary.

Our survey also revealed a considerable level of self-employment in the four study areas. Overall, three out of ten workers were self-employed, with proportions ranging from 22 per cent in the Teifi Valley to 38.1 per cent of workers in the Betws-y-coed study area. This is higher than the average for rural Wales, and indicates that in the more rural areas, self-employment is likely to be even more significant than it is in rural Wales as a whole. Those study areas with the highest levels of self-employment (Betws-y-coed, Devil's Bridge and Tanat Valley) appear to be characterized by above-average levels of farming-related employment, and literary and related employment. Although occupational groups cannot be disag-gregated to reveal individual jobs, it seems reasonable to suggest that these findings confirm previous studies of rural self-employment, namely that it comprises such occupations as farming, crafts, small shops, hotels, and painting, decorating, plumbing and small-scale building work.

Another issue of particular interest, given the efforts of development agencies to promote indigenous enterprise and to 'plug in' rural areas to urban-based service markets through the introduction of appropriate technology, is the degree to which persons in employment work from home. Such 'homeworking' – related to the farming, craft and hospitality/tourism sectors – accounted for almost three out of ten persons in employment, ranging from 16.8 per cent in Devil's Bridge to 41.3 per cent of workers in the Teifi Valley (the study area where farming was most dominant). These are not the 'wired-in' information-technology workers at the forefront of the next economic revolution, but farmers, bed-and-breakfast houses and small businesses trying to cut down on costs by running from home. Homework here is done from necessity rather than by choice, and the high-powered executives and managers who work from their fully electronic offices at home were conspicuous by their absence.

Work issues in rural Wales

These types of employment trends in rural areas have been linked with the identification of particular employment problems. Thus, apart from the persistent problem of a lack of local job opportunities and job choices for many rural people, especially school-leavers (see Stern and Turbin, 1986), the key problems usually identified are:

- the nature of new jobs, which are often poorly paid, insecure, seasonal or part-time;
- the gendering of much new employment, with jobs often being targeted at, and taken up by, women (Little 1987);
- the lack of child-care facilities to permit more child-carers (almost exclusively women) to work (Little, Ross and Collins, 1991);
- inadequate public transport services to reach jobs in nearby urban centres.

Whilst specific local employment initiatives have been undertaken in some of our study areas, it is nevertheless the case that most commentators would agree with Champion and Watkins (1991, 11) who suggest that

These new sources of growth have ... by no means solved the rural employment problems caused by the contraction of traditional industries.

Our survey, which also included a series of questions on the nature of employment problems in each study area, tended to confirm this view. Perhaps the most severe work-related problem is unemployment. As noted earlier in the chapter, unemployment varies greatly in rural Wales, and our survey areas again confirm the general trends. Devil's Bridge and the Tanat Valley are in the TTWAs of Aberystwyth and Welshpool (although a small part of the latter study area is included in the Wrexham TTWA). The relative size of these towns, together with the strength of their service sector, means that the seasonally unadjusted unemployment rates in these TTWAs were only 6.2 and 3.9 per cent respectively at the beginning of 1996, compared with a Welsh rate of 8.6 per cent. The other two study areas lay in the more rural TTWAs of Conwy and Colwyn (Betws-y-coed) and Cardigan (Teifi Valley), and have higher unemployment rates, as we might expect, at 9.3 and 8.2 per cent respectively.

Alongside the officially recognized unemployed, our survey also uncovered 'hidden' groups who were experiencing employment problems in the Welsh countryside. Such groups include women, particularly those women who had no (or limited) access to the household car, and mothers of young children who could not secure suitable child-care facilities (see Little, 1987). Other groups include persons caring for a dependent relative (again usually women), and disabled residents who were over-reliant on inadequate public transport services. Such groups, although including persons who did not wish to enter the job market, were effectively trapped in the home or the local area, and thus were denied the chance of paid employment outside the home or locality. Although such people may not have been registered as unemployed and may not even have been actively seeking work (since they may have come to accept their restrictive circumstances), they nevertheless represented a group which was experiencing considerable employment disadvantages. In this respect, better child-care facilities, improved public transport services, and a wider choice of jobs in the local area might provide some assistance to 'hidden' groups of this kind.

It was noted above that recent population shifts affecting rural Wales have, to varying degrees, mirrored changes in rural employment structures. Across the four areas of rural Wales, employment-related factors (moving to a new job in the local area) accounted for 15.9 per cent of all stated reasons for in-movement. Such a figure might appear low, but it should be recognized that it relates to reasons behind movement to the local area, and so includes both long- and short-distance moves. Other studies of population in-movement to rural areas seem to indicate that the twin factors of employment and retirement dominate long-distance in-movement, whilst a wider spectrum of factors influences shorter moves, such as housing, pleasant environment, and proximity to friends, relatives and essential services.

Another issue which has arisen from previous research on the in-migration of relatively affluent people into rural areas is the degree to which such in-movement sets off a localized multiplier effect in terms of domestic employment. It has been suggested (see Cloke and Thrift, 1990) that one potential spin-off in the local community is that affluent newcomers will require gardeners, cleaners and nannies. The employment of domestic labour is also significant in terms of the flow of women returning to work. Whereas in rural England, levels of paid domestic labour appeared greatest in the higher-income areas, the pattern of such labour in Wales seemed to be more affected by proportions of retired persons. The Teifi Valley and Betws-y-coed areas, where employment of domestic labour was highest (9.4 and 8.5 per cent respectively), contained the highest proportions of persons aged over sixty-five years. The distribution of paid domestic labour also mirrored variations in household savings, with areas of high household savings again reporting high levels of paid domestic employment in the household.

One of the main reasons for the employment of domestic labour relates to the fact that increasing numbers of women in two-adult households are entering the job market. Such paid domestic labour has, to varying degrees, replaced unpaid domestic work performed previously by women within the household. Increasing the numbers of women engaging in paid employment also has ramifications for other aspects of rural life, since much community work has traditionally been performed by women. Increased participation by women in the labour market was, therefore, having an important knock-on effect regarding the ability of those women to continue their voluntary work in the community.

We also found important gender divisions in the types of employment held by persons in the Welsh study areas. Such divisions are important, given the emphasis in recent rural research and policy on the surge of women entering the labour market. As might be expected, our survey showed that a wider spectrum of occupations was held by male workers. Indeed, over 60 per cent of women in employment worked in one of three sectors: professional and related (34.0 per cent); catering, cleaning, hairdressing and other personal services (17.3 per cent); and clerical and related (13.7 per cent). A higher proportion of men than women were employed in the farming and related (17.3/6.6 per cent), managerial (7.1/2.0 per cent), processing/making/repairing and related (10.6/2.0 per cent), construction (6.4/0.0 per cent) and transport (4.9/0.5 per cent) sectors. A greater proportion of women than men worked in the professional and related (34.0/21.6 per cent) catering/cleaning/hairdressing/other personal services (17.3/4.6 per cent), clerical and related (13.7/2.5 per cent), and selling (11.7/5.3 per cent) sectors.

The journey to work

A crucial component in structuring employment opportunity is the nature of the proposed journey to and from work. In rural areas this component becomes even more crucial, since potential employees lack the extensive public transport networks available in most towns and cities. Our survey confirmed the importance of access to a car for an indivdual's employment chances. In terms of travel-to-work patterns, almost four-fifths of persons in employment worked away from their homes. Of these workers, 83.1 per cent followed a daily commuting pattern to the workplace, a further 5.6 per cent travelled daily but worked for less than five days per week, and 9.1 per cent of workers had a varying journey-to-work pattern. Some commentators on the effects of counter-urbanization on rural areas have attributed much significance to the practice of long-distance commuting. It is argued that people working in urban labour markets will increasingly stay near their jobs during the week, and return for the weekends to their rural, family homes. In view of this emphasis, it is perhaps surprising that in our survey only five people (1.6 per cent) travelled to work on a weekly basis. In the four areas of rural Wales, weekly and monthly commuting appeared most prominent in Betws-y-coed (4.5 per cent), with the other areas having less than 2 per cent of adults in employment away from home following such a commuting pattern.

Very few people travelled to work on public transport – public buses and British Rail each accounting for only 1 per cent of commuter journeys. Another 6 per cent of persons in employment travelled to work on a motorcycle, whilst 1 per cent relied on a bicycle. Whilst the reasons for such a mode of transport are not clear from this question, it is apparent that many workers travelled to work in private cars as a matter of necessity rather than choice. This again confirms the data which are available at regional and national level. In 1991, only 4 per cent of all men's journeys to work in Wales were by bus (Moyes, 1995, 201). Our survey indicates that this figure is probably inflated by urban and suburban commuting, and that in the more rural areas the use of the bus will be considerably lower than this average. The fact that less than 2 per cent of workers travel to work by public transport in such areas raises interesting questions about the role that public transport is playing in rural areas. Furthermore, such a high incidence of reliance on private household vehicles for the journey to work had important consequences for one-car households in which the car was unavailable for other household members during working days. In such households, it was very often the female partner who was forced to rely on either public transport services or lifts from friends and relatives (see also chapter 5 on accessibility).

The fact that such a high percentage of people used cars to commute to work should by no means be taken as an indicator that their journeys were unproblematic, and roughly 61 per cent of those commuting experienced problems. Indeed, most prominent amongst these difficulties, and accounting for about two-thirds of all stated problems, appeared to be an over-reliance placed on private cars. Also of importance, and related to the above difficulty, was a lack of, or inadequate public transport service – which accounted for around 10 per cent of problems mentioned. Bad road conditions comprised a further 7 per cent of stated transport problems, with the price of petrol (1.7 per cent), no work bus (8 per cent) and parking problems (1.5 per cent) making up the remainder of stated difficulties. The difficulties experienced by those travelling to work in rural Wales, even those doing so by car, are emphasized by the fact that the study areas with the highest perceptions of commuting difficulties are also the areas in which commuting itself is at the highest levels.

Finding employment

In some senses we are one step ahead in our discussion, and a consideration of the issues of travelling to work is premised on the fact that an individual has a job to travel to. The two are of course linked at an early stage in the job-seeking procedure in that travelling difficulties may prevent a job being taken up or even applied for. In this section we will broaden the discussion to other aspects of finding a job.

The most frequently cited method by which persons found out about their present job, or previous job if retired, were via advertisements in the local media – accounting for about 21 per cent of all stated methods. A recommendation from a friend and direct personal enquiries were the main methods for about 19 per cent and 14 per cent of people respectively, with a further 8 per cent gaining work via the job centre or an advertisement in the national media. This shows the importance of local networks in rural areas, with over 50 per cent of people having found out about their employment via local press, personal enquiry or friends.

Of those persons in paid employment or self-employed during the previous twelve months, roughly 18 per cent reported that they had experienced difficulties in obtaining the type of job they required in the local area. Such problems appeared to be most apparent in the Devil's Bridge (27.4 per cent) and Teifi Valley (21.5 per cent) areas. The dominant perception of employment disadvantage among respondents related to a restricted range of jobs available in the local area – accounting for almost 50 per cent of all stated difficulties. Linking back to the previous section, this factor meant that many residents were forced to commute considerable distances to work, which, when combined with inadequate public transport services, necessitated the ownership of a private vehicle. Other respondents identified some key characteristics of rural employment that served to disadvantage many residents currently in work, or actively seeking employment – low pay, the seasonal nature of farming and tourism-based employment, and weekly commuting.

The experience of employment disadvantage

Across the four study areas of rural Wales an average of over 75 per cent of respondents considered that there were particular disadvantages connected with employment in the local area. Such high levels of awareness of employment disadvantage appeared to be related more to issues of underemployment, low pay, restricted choice of jobs, and inadequate public transport than to actual unemployment. These perceived employment problems were most prominent in the Devil's Bridge and Tanat Valley study areas, whilst less frequently mentioned in Betws-y-coed.

The remainder of this chapter focuses on comments provided by respondents and key interview contacts on the nature of and problems associated with employment in the study areas. Since such comments were recorded verbatim by the interviewer, they provide a valuable source of opinion on the topic. From the 1,000 household interviews and study-visit reports we have selected a small sample of the comments which reflect some of the interpretations of the data tabulated above. For example many respondents commented that a limited range of local jobs represented the main employment problem in their area. Such a factor meant that many local people were forced to travel considerable distances to their place of work. Such long-distance commuting, when combined with inadequate public transport services, required private transport:

You have to travel outside the locality if you want to find a job of any sort. (1122, Betws-y-coed)

Living far out. No bus route. Hard to find a job. (2119, Devil's Bridge)

There's no local work. All [my] daughters have had to go to Oswestry to be secretaries. (3034, Tanat Valley)

There is absolutely nothing available. Must be prepared to travel. (3026, Tanat Valley)

Problems of transport preventing people starting businesses here. (4128, Teifi Valley)

Respondents identified some key characteristics of local employment that served to disadvantage many residents currently in work or actively seeking employment: the seasonal nature of agricultural and tourism-based employment, low pay, weekly commuting and unemployment:

[No] ... full-time jobs. Betws-y-coed is a tourist place, forestry, etc. Only in summer is plenty of work available. (1122, Betws-y-coed)

Very limited types of work available and not much of what there is and the pay is crap. (2196, Devil's Bridge)

Several husbands have moved away to get work and come home at weekends. (Betws-y-coed clerk)

So many on the dole. No work in the district. Have to go to different places. (4088, Teifi Valley)

Our respondents pinpointed specific groups of people – professionals, the elderly, young people and women – who had very real problems in finding jobs in the study areas. A number of respondents in several areas commented that professional or qualified people found it particularly difficult to find suitable work in the local area, and either had to take a local job for which they were over-qualified or move elsewhere for a suitable job:

Lack of suitable employment [for] skilled people. (1205, Betws-y-coed)

People with qualifications have to go to Shrewsbury or Welshpool or Oswestry. (3057, Tanat Valley)

People moving out are those that are going to university. The types of jobs that they're going to get – well, they're not going to want to come back to Llanrhaeadr. (Tanat Valley clerk)

Young people, particularly those without skills, training or qualifications were also seen as disadvantaged in terms of job opportunities:

No work for youngsters. (2184, Devil's Bridge)

No work for school-leavers. No major employers. Only one hotel. (3222, Tanat Valley)

Women represented another group perceived as facing particular problems finding jobs in the area, and comments from respondents illustrate particular groups of women who are experiencing employment-related difficulties and the characteristics of the problems faced by them:

Not much employment for housewives who need part-time work. (1146, Betws-y-coed)

Women with children [experience problems]. (2200, Devil's Bridge)

Finally, several respondents mentioned the inevitability of young people leaving the area for job-related reasons. From various sections of the household questionnaire it was apparent that a restricted range of local employment was the single most important reason why young people were moving out of rural areas:

Most people commute [to work] and the youngsters move away. (Betws-y-coed clerk)

Young people tend to move out of the village to at least as far off as Llanrwst to find work. It is difficult to work in the village. (1104, Betws-y-coed)

I think employment is the main reason for people moving out. (Teifi Valley clerk)

Conclusion

At the beginning of this chapter we raised a number of questions about the problems of rural employment that had not yet been solved by rural development policy responses in Wales. The evidence presented here from our surveys suggests that rural people perceived employment problems as an important issue. The fact that a range of 51–81 per cent of respondents considered both that particular groups of rural people were experiencing difficulties in gaining employment in the study areas, and that there were significant employment disadvantages in the area, is evidence of a strong body of local opinion and provides a platform for an argument which suggests that even more should be done to alleviate these problems. The evidence presented in this chapter reinforces the presupposition that the restructuring of the rural economy has been accompanied by a continuation of long-standing problems of employment and underemployment, and that many rural jobs, especially in the more peripheral areas, are in sectors where seasonal, part-time and insecure work represents a significant element of overall employment.

The ability of rural residents to gain access to jobs was in many cases severely restricted by a lack of transport. This represents a potential cumulative problem for residents with low, or no, income and, therefore, unable to afford the purchase and running costs of a vehicle of their own. Even with some private transport, however, the numbers and types of jobs available in rural areas presented very difficult problems for young people, older people, women and those seeking professionally qualified work. Other associated issues of low pay are discussed in chapter 6.

The traditional wisdom of existing analyses of rural employment problems (see Cloke, 1993) suggests that economic development policy has become too focused and that more rural areas should become eligible for the activities and funds which are currently attracted to DBRW and WDA areas and European Commission Objective 5b areas. Despite the fact that each of our study areas qualifies for public funds via one or more of these agencies, the evidence presented here confirms that important problems persist in each area despite the best efforts of local and national agencies to improve the situation. Any spreading of resources to other areas will have obvious implications for the future of those areas already identified as worthy of agency attention.

There is, however, also the problem of using the existing policies to the best effect. Even though much of rural Wales qualifies for European structural fund support as an Objective 5b area, the number of locations which actually benefit from these funds is fairly small. There is a tendency to concentrate funds in and around the larger towns, which means that those without ready access again fail to benefit. Thus, for instance, new leisure centres have been supported in Aberystwyth, Barmouth, Brecon, Llangefni,

Machynlleth and Pwllheli to a total amount of £6.2 million, and Bala has received aid worth £1.75 million to develop tourism around its lake. Existing funds, crucial as they are, also tend to be for very specific purposes, and thus by definition can only reach particular places and particular groups of people. Thus several areas in west Wales benefited from KONVER grants to assist the diversification of the local economy following the contraction of the defence industry in the late 1980s and early 1990s. The four LEADER groups, set up in 1991 to establish and introduce business plans to regenerate their local economies, shared an allocation of £2.34 million, and these and a further four were funded in 1994 under LEADER II for an additional £7 million. Parts of mid-Wales benefit from the RETEX initiative which gives grants in order to accelerate the diversification of economic activity in areas heavily dependent on textiles and clothing, and a large part of rural Wales also receives funds from the Common Agricultural Policy as an Objective 5a area.

There is therefore a very large amount of state assistance currently coming into rural Wales, especially from the EU, which is specifically targeted at improving the rural economy. One concern is that such funds need to be increasingly co-ordinated and integrated (see Blackaby et al., 1995, 291-3). There is a particular need for the agricultural funds to be seen as part of a broader package of rural development, and for the economic and social impacts of the structural funds to be evaluated in tandem.

These debates, however, important as they are, sometimes seem to miss out on what the structuring of employment opportunities actually means to rural people experiencing development-related problems. Recent suggestions of high suicide rates among farmers being related to financial difficulties associated with current economic restructuring, provide an extreme but important example of the more human aspects of these 'problems'.

It is sometimes assumed that if unemployment, underemployment or low-pay conditions are to some extent unavoidable, then it is better to be jobless or poor in the countryside, which offers environmental and community compensations. However, by the same (arguable) token, the lack of anonymity and the potential loneliness of rural living may have the opposite effect, and rural lifestyles may lead to experiences of entrapment or hopelessness rather than offering a compensatory lifestyle. These issues are further considered in chapter 6, when the question of low income is addressed more directly. It remains the case though, that the links between work and other aspects of rural lifestyle discussed elsewhere in the book are crucial to an understanding of how structured rural opportunities and experiences of rural life interconnect.

References

Archbishop's Commission on Rural Areas (1990) *Faith in the Countryside*, Churchman, Worthing.

Blackaby, D., Murphy, P., O'Leary, N., and Thomas, E. (1995) 'Wales: an economic survey', *Contemporary Wales*, 8, 213-95.

Blunden, J. and Curry, N. (1988) *A Future for our Countryside?* Blackwell, Oxford.

Champion, T. and Watkins, C. (eds.) (1991) *People in the Countryside* Paul Chapman, London.

Cloke, P. (1987) 'Rurality and change: some cautionary notes', *Journal of Rural Studies*, 3, 71-6.

Cloke, P. (1989) 'Rural geography and political economy' in R. Peet and N. Thrift (eds.), *New Models in Geography*, Unwin Hyman, London.

Cloke, P. (1993) 'On "problems and solutions": the reproduction of problems for rural communities in Britain during the 1980s', *Journal of Rural Studies*, 9, 113-23.

Cloke, P. and Thrift, N. (1990) 'Class and change in rural Britain', in T. Marsden, P. Lowe and S. Whatmore (eds.), *Rural Restructuring*, Fulton, London.

Central Statistical Office, (1992) *Social Trends*, HMSO, London.

European Commission (1995) *The Regions of the United Kingdom*, HMSO, London.

Fothergill, S. and Gudgin, G. (1982) *Unequal Growth*, Heinemann, London.

Gilg, A. (1991) *Countryside Planning Policies for the 1990s*, CAB International, Wallingford.

Hodge, I. and Monk, S. (1987) 'Manufacturing employment change within rural areas', *Journal of Rural Studies*, 3, 65-70.

Keeble, D. (1984) 'The urban–rural manufacturing shift', *Geography*, 69, 163-6.

Little, J. (1987) 'Gender relations in rural areas: the importance of women's domestic role', *Journal of Rural Studies*, 3, 335-42.

Little, J., Ross, K. and Collins, I. (1991) *Women and Employment in Rural Areas*, RDC, London.

Moyes, T. (1995) 'Local bus services in Wales: changing supply patterns since deregulation', *Contemporary Wales*, 8, 183-211.

Office of Population and Census Surveys (1980) *Classification of Occupations,* OPCS, London.

PA Cambridge Consultants (1992) *Business Success in the Countryside,* HMSO, London.

Robinson, G. (1990) *Conflict and Change in the Countryside,* Belhaven, London.

Sandefur, G. (1988) 'Blacks, Hispanics, American Indians and poverty – and what worked', in F. Harris and R. Wilkins (eds.), *Quiet Riots,* Pantheon, New York.

Stern, E. and Turbin, J. (1986) *Youth Employment and Unemployment in Rural England,* RDC, London.

Thrift, N. (1987) 'Manufacturing rural geography?', *Journal of Rural Studies,* 3, 77–82.

Welsh Office (1996) *A Working Countryside for Wales,* Cm. 3180, HMSO, London.

5 • Accessibility and Services

Introduction

Post-war studies of rural change have focused considerable attention on the decline of rural transport. Early syntheses (see Clout, 1972) emphasised the Beeching cuts in the rural rail network, and the shrinking commercial viability of rural bus services. By 1979, in a book of the same title, Moseley was able to nominate 'Accessibility' as '*the* rural challenge'. Public transport was increasingly subject to route reduction, patronage reduction and fare increases, and even though significant government subsidies were attracted to these services, the competition between public transport and private car ownership was one-sided in favour of the car (Banister, 1980). Thus the 'link' between rural people and the services, facilities, jobs and other opportunities required for a good standard of rural lifestyle became increasingly eroded for those who were non-mobile by dint of poverty, age, infirmity, disability or gender.

Given this erosion, accessibility, or rather lack of it, became one of the key defining components of rural deprivation. In an extremely influential paper also published in 1979, Shaw suggested three categories of deprivation which might combine in rural areas to produce a self-sustaining spiral of disadvantage (see also chapter 6 for more details of the deprivation debate). These were;

(1) Household deprivation: problems relating to criteria such as income and housing which dictate the ability of individuals to make use of those opportunities that are available in rural areas.
(2) Opportunity deprivation: problems relating to the loss of particular facets of rural life, such as jobs and services, from their previous rural location.
(3) Mobility deprivation: problems stemming from the inability of some rural people to gain access to jobs, services and facilities which have moved away from village locations.

Shaw's thesis was that the low incomes of those suffering from household deprivation, would in turn lead them to suffer increased opportunity and mobility deprivation. Mobility deprivation, or lack of accessibility, would in turn reduce opportunities, which would themselves impact upon household incomes – and the cycle would continue in this self-reinforcing manner. The contribution to this cycle made by a lack of accessibility in rural areas is far more crucial than in urban areas. As Nutley explains (1984, 12),

> Accessibility ... is the purpose of transport, and consequently 'problems' should be understood in terms of difficulties of acquiring the degrees of access felt to be necessary ... The situation is distinctly more simple in rural areas than in urban, where there is a much greater range of services and facilities, and alternative destinations, routes and transport modes. In urban cases, the ability to acquire access to desirable services would almost always be possible, and relative accessibility would have to be expressed in terms of time, or cost, or both ... In rural areas however, and especially in the more sparsely populated ones such as rural Wales, the available facilities are so widely dispersed and remaining transport services so frugal, that the crucial issue becomes whether access is possible at all.

Thus in rural areas, the combined effect of household, opportunity and mobility deprivation was seen as isolating particular groups within rural communities and presenting them with complex and sometimes insurmountable difficulties in obtaining the basic needs for survival in their established place of residence. These difficulties are cumulative for the individuals and households concerned, and are often hidden in the rural environment: unemployment levels, poverty, poor living conditions, social stress and isolation in small and scattered communities remain hidden out of sight and out of mind, compared with the immediacy and scale of similar afflictions in urban environments.

Shaw's analysis was useful, at least in part, because it was found to be politically expedient by local government agencies for furthering their own objectives. However, far from being a springboard to further investigations of who were the 'deprived', what exactly their problems were, and why these problems were occurring, Shaw's categories were used as a focus of investigations into rural deprivation which became bogged down by the notion that it was service provision which was paramount in rural areas, and that poor levels of provision reflected an urban bias in allocations of expenditure to local authorities (see Association of County Councils, 1979; Association of District Councils, 1978). The provision of public transport, and the politics surrounding it, became a key part of this debate, so further cementing the issue of accessibility into the accepted discourses of rural deprivation.

Accessibility has thus been established as a subject encompassing the connections between the triple factors of person, link and activity in rural lifestyles. Each of these factors is subject to change. The types of people in rural areas are subject to flux, particularly because of in-migration (often of affluent and mobile people) and the ageing of existing populations (often becoming decreasingly mobile). The activity base at a local scale is also changing, with a long history of service rationalization in both public- and private-sector services (see Cloke, 1986) and the diminution of *in situ* service levels in rural settlements. Such changes necessitate trips to larger places for an increasing number of residents in order to gain access to necessary goods, services and facilities. The transport link has also continued to change, most recently with the introduction of privatization and deregulation into the public transport sector, first in the case of buses (see Bell and Cloke, 1990, 1991) and latterly with the proposals for the sell-off of rail services. Such changes in accessibility connections have been the source of concern over a long period of time, and for many rural agencies such concerns have heightened, and not abated:

> For many of the newcomers, and some of their long established neighbours, [the disappearance of rural services] may be merely an inconvenience. But for elderly people living alone, mothers with young children, people with disabilities and unemployed or otherwise disadvantaged people, such an environment constitutes real deprivation. The spaciousness of the countryside is a delight for some ... and a prison for others. (M. Moseley, ACRE Annual Report 1992)

Public policy has at various stages in the last thirty years been focused on all three aspects of the accessibility connections:

- *People* have been encouraged to live in concentrated settlements rather than scattered throughout the countryside (the so-called key settlement policies; see Cloke 1979, 1983).
- *Services and facilities* have been delivered as locally as possible, although recent expenditure restrictions have led to a rationalization of most public services into larger settlements.
- *Transport links* have received long-standing subsidies.

Our research, therefore, aimed to investigate a number of key issues relating to accessibility problems in rural areas:

- the scope of public transport services
- the availability of private transport (at household and individual levels)
- the incidence of 'non-mobile' individuals or groups who were dependent on public transport or lift-giving
- the experiences of non-mobility as part of a rural lifestyle
- the changing nature of local services
- how such services are reached by local people
- the experiences of living in a poorly serviced environment.

In each case, different groups of people are identified as having experience of particular problems associated with changes in the 'links' and the activities of rural accessibility.

Transport

Transport must be considered to be the most significant factor in terms of isolation and access, particularly in the context of the low level of fixed local service provision which is found in peripheral areas such as rural Wales. In order to offer lifestyle choices, access to alternative services must be made available to the rural population if those services are not within their everyday environment. It is easy to dismiss this as a private concern, given the high levels of private car ownership in rural Wales. The 1991 Census figures for Wales suggest that only 32.3 per cent of households had no car, whilst 22.1 per cent had two or more. It is generally accepted that the level of car ownership is highest in rural areas (Robinson 1990, 352), so we may expect car ownership levels in the region of 70–80 per cent. However, the experience of isolation from services, employment, leisure facilities, and friends or relatives is not so easily dismissed for the significant minority of the rural population who do not have everyday access to affordable personal transport.

Several studies have established that significant parts of rural Wales are indeed locations where such isolation is still a large problem. After a major research project carried out for the Welsh Office at the beginning of the 1980s, Nutley was forced to conclude that access standards for non-car owners in rural Wales are frequently poor, and and in many cases very poor. (1984, 29; see also Nutley, 1982, 1983; Cloke 1984; Moyes 1989)

More recent research by Moyes on the effects of the 1985 Transport Act which deregulated local bus services, indicates that

in rural areas ... the perceived quality gap between bus and personal motorized mobility continues to widen.

This is as we might expect, for as Bell and Cloke have pointed out, following their study of the initial effects of bus deregulation in Powys,

In rural areas such as mid Wales ... deregulation has not sparked off competition, because the least populated areas do not represent good profit for new investors in the sector. Therefore the 'benefits' of deregulation are least in evidence in these marginal areas. (1989, 12)

This is certainly borne out by the results of our survey where we asked households if they thought local public transport services had improved or deteriorated over the last five years. There was an overall perception that transport services had deteriorated, and in each study area, more people perceived transport services to have deteriorated than improved, with highest rates of perceived decline reported in the study areas of Teifi Valley (37.2 per cent) and Tanat Valley (31.0 per cent). We can draw three main conclusions from this. First, it is important to note that not all residents were living in a world where they perceived public transport decline. It seems likely that the realignments of rural populations have altered the expectations of both long-term rural residents and newcomers alike, with respect to the levels of 'local' service provision. There is also the possibility that limited 'first-hand' experiences of the services concerned may lead to respondents inferring an improvement or deterioration from an interpretation of reported national trends. Secondly, the overall (and overwhelming) weight of opinion was that transport services had declined over recent years. Thirdly, when we correlate these responses with the levels of car ownership in each area, we find that an exact determination of the relationship between poor public transport services and high private transport use (or vice versa) is difficult. It may have been the case that poor (or expensive) public transport had forced people into private transport use, or that good public provision had lessened the requirement for private vehicles. Conversely, it is possible that increasing private transport had reduced the requirement and use of public transport, so that the public transport provision was proportionally reduced, or even withdrawn. Whatever the exact nature of this relationship, respondents were still aware of the responsibilities of public transport provision.

The most frequently recorded comments regarding the disadvantage of the area, and indeed in expressing what made the area rural, included allusion to the necessity of private transport, and the physical isolation of the location.

If you haven't got a car it's harder to get around. The buses don't run often enough. There's a lot of waiting around. (2194, Devil's Bridge)

[The main disadvantage of this area is] isolation with no personal transport. (3054, Tanat Valley)

Buses – very poor, one a week goes to Llanrwst . . . It's far from everywhere and there's no public services. Unless you've got a car it's a very inconvenient place to live. (Betws-y-coed clerk)

[The disadvantage of this area is] . . . people living in the country without transport. They manage all right because they arrange their lives around the fact that there's a bus going to Cardigan on a Friday, so they go shopping on a Friday. (Teifi Valley clerk)

These experiences suggest both a marginalization of the transport-poor and evidence of a range of coping strategies employed to channel accessibility into available times and routes (however sparse). Given this context, it is interesting that a significant minority of 5 per cent overall reported no local bus service at all. Here we have to take account of different definitions of 'local' and of the likelihood that a 'no' answer to this question could stem, for example, from either highly mobile people who have no need of a local bus service and, therefore, no knowledge of it, or from non-mobile people whose awareness of the lack of a service is acute precisely because of their need for it. The proportion of respondents reporting the absence of a local bus service ranged from 1.8 per cent in Devil's Bridge to 6.0 per cent in the Teifi Valley study area.

This information should be considered in conjunction with that gained when we asked respondents about the frequency of local bus services. Here again, the widely varying reports of frequency could suggest a number of different types of services in different places, or a situation in which many local people have no detailed knowledge of when their local bus services run.

In aggregate, our responses suggest that the Teifi Valley had the highest frequency of perceived provision, with 54.5 per cent of respondents reporting a bus at least every two hours. In the Tanat Valley, by contrast, it appears that most residents had to rely on only one or two buses per day, with a significant minority (14.3 per cent) reporting a bus service on just two to three days per week. Of note was the ignorance of bus timetabling by a large minority of the sample (from 15.7 per cent in the Tanat Valley to 44.5 per cent in Betws-y-coed), which might suggest a high level of reliance on private transport. This too was evidenced by some of the comments from our respondents:

> Better bus service [needed] – but are there enough customers? (3201, Tanat Valley)

Whilst acknowledging that the lack of transport caused serious problems for a minority of residents, community council representatives sometimes took a pragmatic view of rural transport provision.

> How much these services are used is another problem. (Teifi Valley clerk)

> Demise of the local bus service because people use cars. (Teifi Valley clerk)

However, in some areas the poor patronage of public transport may have had explanations other than apathy or low demand.

> The buses are regular . . . but they get to Aberystwyth and . . . have to be there for a very short or very long time. (Devil's Bridge clerk)

> They have to depend on others because the bus service is awful, especially at holiday times when the school bus doesn't run. (Devil's Bridge clerk)

> There's a few more buses in the summer. (Betws-y-coed clerk)

These last comments also highlight a transport problem associated with areas of high tourist interest and very seasonal activity. The permanent residents of any such area have benefited from any intensive service provided for the tourists, but have suffered from the drop-off in provision in low season. Those in lower income brackets would appear most vulnerable in this situation, particularly as the costs of maintaining private transport are year-round, so that alternatives may not be instantly available in winter.

Since public transport services tend to be infrequent and sometimes inconvenient in most of the study areas, the issue of levels of ownership of private transport is important in assessing overall levels of accessibility in rural areas. Our questionnaire did not ask about the level of car ownership in the household, but instead asked which household members had access to a vehicle. Single or multiple car ownership cannot be inferred from this question, since respondents may have regarded each household member as having access to a shared vehicle. Information from the 1991 Census does however offer some context for this question, and this confirms the suggestion made in the introduction to this chapter that there exist relatively high levels of vehicle ownership in rural areas – with an average of 82.5 per cent of households in our study areas having access to at least one vehicle, compared with 67.7 per cent for Wales as a whole. Levels of car ownership as reported in the Census ranged from 79.0 per cent in Betws-y-coed to 87.8 per cent in the Devil's Bridge study area. Just under a third of households in our study areas were also reported as having two or more cars – again confirming the importance of the car to rural households. The average access to a car for our study areas was 63.7 per cent of households, a rate much below the mean for the four comparable areas of rural England (74.9 per cent). This again masks geographical variation, with the 34.6 per cent difference between the highest (Tanat Valley) and lowest (Teifi Valley) rates extremely significant. We have to conclude from all this information that there were very significant pockets of non-mobile households in rural Wales who were not served by frequent bus services.

It also becomes apparent that access to a vehicle varied considerably *within* households. We found that 30.4 per cent of people in Betws-y-coed, 25.8 per cent in the Tanat Valley, 22.9 per cent in the Teifi Valley and 18.2 per cent of persons in Devil's Bridge had no access to a vehicle at certain times of day. Here, the 'classic' situation is that the (usually male) main earner took the car to work, leaving the (usually female) 'other' member of the household non-mobile in the home location, often with young children to look after. It seems most likely that this scenario is too simplistic an account of the rather complex nature of household participation in, and trips to, the local labour market, but even so, there is still likely to be a gendered difference in access to the only car in many households.

An obvious but sometimes forgotten aspect of access to privately owned vehicles is the ability to drive, and as with the previous indicator, we identified a high proportion of people living in the Welsh study areas who held no driving licence (19.3 per cent). This represented a high level of dependency on public or voluntary transport to gain access to services and facilities which are not *in situ*, and places heavy emphasis on the need to sustain viable *local* services in these areas.

By juxtaposing data on income with those on car access, we assessed the possibility that the situation in which household members had no access to a vehicle at some times of the day may be connected to low income levels in the areas concerned. Broadly there seemed to be a connection between low levels of access to a vehicle and higher levels of low-income households in only the Betws-y-coed area. However, it might be suggested that access levels are not necessarily dictated by rigid economic or geographical factors. There would appear to be a considerable number of 'reluctant car owners' amongst the poorer groups in all areas for whom private accessibility had become a genuine necessity, so other economic sacrifices may be made in people's lifestyles in order to accommodate these necessary costs. Thus, rather than there being a simple relationship between low income and car access, the social dimensions of age, gender, infirmity and so on also appeared to be influential in determining who did not own or drive a vehicle, although of course low incomes continued to be a constraining factor.

Inaccessibility, or isolation, remained a very important problem for some people in rural Wales. Isolation must be considered to be a problem for those who have no access to a vehicle some or all of the time, and for those without driving licences who must rely on the good will and prior commitments of others (either within a household or neighbours, friends or relatives) to gain access to transport, or have the time and money to utilize public transport. These constraints were usually made more acute by the inappropriate timing of bus journeys (where they existed at all) for social and leisure activities, and sometimes for work as well. This was frequently seen as a problem for the young (in terms of social life) and the old (in terms of health requirements).

Need a late bus, weekdays for teenagers. (2023, Devil's Bridge)

[A disadvantage] for someone without transport, particularly if they're old or infirm. (1009, Betws-y-coed)

These findings again mirror those of earlier studies of transport in rural Wales. Moyes in particular, in his work on unmet need, identified similar categories of people who were especially hard hit by a lack of suitable public transport services – children who needed to be mobile, perhaps for after-school activities, but who were of pre-driving age, and those who needed to travel to and from hospital and day-care centres (1989, 21–4).

These social differentiations in access to private transport are shown in more detail when we take the single axis of gender. The difference across all four areas of the survey between males and females having no access to a vehicle was 10.2 per cent for men and 17.6 per cent for women. In other words, nearly twice as many women did not have access to a vehicle. Again, there was considerable geographical variation in this differentiation. The largest differential was in Betws-y-coed, with 23.4 per cent of women without access, as opposed to 11.0 per cent of men. The Devil's Bridge study area appeared to have the lowest rate of non-access for women at 12.0 per cent, and for men at 3.3 per cent. Possession of a driving licence also showed gender differences. Across the four study areas, 26.1 per cent of woman had no licence, compared with only 8.8 per cent of men. As we have already noted, however, even holding a licence was no guarantee of mobility. The contradictions of reported access and the non-holding of a licence, especially for women (e.g. Tanat Valley at 14.6 per cent and 31.0 per cent respectively) may indicate the assumed reliance of non-licence holders being granted access to transport whenever they request it. Given the differential activity patterns experienced within households, the reality may not accord with such an assumption.

For those without access to a motor vehicle, the most common form of mobility was by foot. This information is important because it begins to offer an insight into the lifestyle of non-mobile groups in rural areas. Overall, 37.8 per cent of our respondents without a car made their 'link' with services and facilities by foot, although in the Teifi Valley slightly more people use a bus than walk, and in Devil's Bridge the numbers using these two modes are equal. This has implications for the type and length of journeys undertaken, the obvious one being that those without cars are restricted to nearby local destinations. A reliance on walking also militates against the elderly and the infirm, and rural life for some continues to involve the difficult and isolating process of 'getting about' without a car. In the light of this, the fact that almost twice as many people in Betws-y-coed and the Tanat Valley walk instead of using a bus indicates severely restricted mobility. The level of rail use is extremely low in each of the study areas, confirming the impression of rural Wales as being very poorly served by train.

There has been much speculation by rural researchers that problems of non-mobility in rural areas are being overcome informally by people obtaining lifts from family and friends and by sharing cars. There is some evidence of this in the answers given to us about alternative transport for those with no car, and these informal mechanisms for access were undoubtedly important in some areas – particularly the Teifi Valley (27.4 per cent) and Betws-y-coed (17.2 per cent). However, not as many people as we expected were using these informal mechanisms, and the overwhelming conclusion to draw from this section of the survey is that over a third of those without a car are walking to services and facilities, pointing to the severe restrictions on accessibility and mobility that are faced by a very significant minority of those in rural Wales.

Services

Studies of rural services over the last two or three decades (e.g. Standing Conference of Rural Community Councils, 1978; Clark and Woollett, 1990; Lievesley and Maynard, 1992) have painted a bleak picture of the rationalization of private- and public-sector services away from small rural locations and into larger centres. Villages have been seen to lose their shops, post offices, primary schools and health services, in many cases despite vigorous political lobbying for the retention of public services and 'use it or lose it' campaigns for local shops. This is certainly the case in rural Wales, where a report by the DBRW in 1993 found that in 185 settlements with a population of less than 3,000, 66 per cent lacked a permanent shop, 21 per cent had no post office, 31 per cent did not have a primary school and 15 per cent were without a bus service (Blackaby et al., 1995, 275). Recently mooted changes to the methods of paying pensions and benefits, and the proposed privatization of post offices are seen as the latest threats to sustaining the post office/shop in rural locations.

In addition to asking our respondents about the quality of their transport services, we also asked about their perceptions of improvements or deteriorations in a range of other services over the previous five years. The responses offer an interesting mix of overall perceptions of improvement and decline. Shops and post offices were viewed overall as subject to continued deterioration, whereas schools and health services were thought to have improved. There were, however, even in many cases where deterioration in service provision was noted, some significant minorities reporting service improvements. These important findings should be placed in the context of the recent deceleration of school and cottage hospital closures (the bulk of such closures took place earlier than the mid-1980s) and a continuing recomposition of rural society with new in-movers tending to accept the existing service structure they encountered as 'normal' for a rural area. Such rural residents tended to be sufficiently affluent and/or mobile to travel to other service locations. Any improvement in the apparent quality of services thereby creates an impression of overall local service improvement without reference to the previously more dense distribution of services in rural areas. It is reasonable to suggest that as more people become accustomed to these new service environments, the problems encountered by non-mobile and low-income households become more deeply hidden in the overall impressions of rural lifestyles. A more detailed investigation of individual services throws more light on these themes.

Shops and post offices

Our responses show that as a mean across the four study areas, more households reported a decline over the last five years in shop (26.9 per cent) and post office (15.9 per cent) services than felt that these had improved. This does mask some considerable variation across the study areas, however, with a higher proportion of respondents in the Teifi Valley reporting shop services as having improved, whilst slightly more respondents in the Devil's Bridge study area considered that post office services had improved than reported a deterioration. Perceived decline amongst shop services was greatest in the Betws-y-coed (33.3 per cent) and the Tanat Valley (31.3 per cent) study areas, and deterioration in post office services was reported by a higher proportion of respondents in the Teifi Valley (19.5 per cent) and Betws-y-coed (18.2 per cent) study areas. Again, it is worth noting that a majority of respondents in each study area reported that the provision of such services had not changed over recent years, or felt that they were not in a position to comment (having lived in the area for a relatively short period of time).

The accessibility of retail services is crucial to those living in a rural area. There are still many people whose lives are centred on the more peripheral rural areas, despite the numbers whose work takes them into towns on a daily basis. In the expenditure section of the questionnaire an attempt was made to determine the use of local (including mobile) shops, and places of more specialized shopping. Our survey also asked about the difficulties encountered in using the local post office, and almost 10 per cent of respondents indicated that they did experience some form of difficulty in this respect, either in terms of access or in opening times. When asking about shopping for everyday needs, we found that this took place at the local shop for an average of 40.4 per cent of respondent households across the four study areas, with the Tanat Valley recording the highest use level at just under a half (49.0 per cent). Shops in the nearest larger town were used for their everyday needs by the largest number of people in the Devil's Bridge (61.5 per cent) and Teifi Valley (37.4 per cent) study areas, whilst a further 25 per cent of those in the Teifi Valley used another town (probably Carmarthen) for their everyday needs. We also asked people the reason why respondents did not use their local shop. As might be expected, the issue of high prices compared with elsewhere was an important consideration for many people, as were other attractions of larger stores which could offer more choice and were possibly located in a common destination for the households concerned. Many people cited 'other' reasons for not using the local shop, particularly in the Teifi Valley, and this may reflect the lack of attachment of some newer residents to traditional community values which include – and for some are symbolized by – use of the village shop, or it may reflect the fact that there was no local shop. As one of our interviewees stated:

> There's nothing [in the village] at the moment, but there was a small grocery shop. (Tanat Valley clerk)

The quality and clarity of information about shopping at different levels of settlement hierarchies is often beset by difficulties over what constitutes the 'nearest town' and so on. In this survey, respondents were left to define such terms themselves, and so the idea of the 'nearest town' should be viewed in conjunction with the location of the study areas, and should be interpreted as the next nearest town to the place of residence for the household. As some respondents lived in larger settlements than others, such definitional issues will themselves provoke an apparent diversity in answers to questions about shopping locations, but we suspect that the question is straightforward to rural residents themselves.

The majority of respondents reported that they undertook specialized shopping in another town. The use of such shops varied from 61.2 per cent in Betws-y-coed to 40.2 per cent in the Devil's Bridge study area. If specialized shopping did not take place in an 'other town', it tended to be done in the nearest town, rather than locally or by mail order. This again underlines the importance of access to these towns, although specialized shopping will obviously have occurred less frequently than that for everyday needs.

Perhaps the most robust and significant conclusion that may be drawn from these particular tables is that the majority of shopping was not done locally. Whilst much specialist shopping might be expected to be done elsewhere, the low figures for everyday purchases seem indicative of ever-increasing large town/out-of-town shopping practices. This distinction was blurred because, despite the apparent success of out-of-town retail outlets, responses for these as places of usual shopping are low. However, the fact that the 'shop in the nearest town' might also be an 'out-of-town super-market' confuses the issue. It seems reasonable to assert that if those who do have multiple-vehicle access within a household maintain such shopping practices, the village shop becomes less and less viable in economic terms. In the event of closure of such facilities, the minority who rely on the local shop as a source of everyday items and as a social focus will become considerably more isolated than their more mobile neighbours, even in less remote rural areas. As one community council clerk stated,

> There's nothing in Llandyfriog . . . [and in] Adpar [the] butcher [and the] village shop closed down. People have to travel . . . The ideal situation is that you've got a car and [then] there's no problem. (Teifi Valley clerk)

Mobile shops were once seen as a crucial way of responding to such closures, and we asked our respondents whether they made regular use of mobile shops. Overall, 21.0 per cent of respondents reported a frequent use of mobile retail outlets, with the greatest level of use recorded in the Teifi Valley (33.7 per cent). Conversely, only 2.9 per cent used such facilities in the Tanat Valley. Not only does this point to the very localized experience of mobility and accessibility problems, but we believe that it is also an important indicator of significant groups of non-mobile people who continue to rely on the mobility of services to reach them because they often do not have the mobility to reach the services. Despite the much-publicized increase in the number of mobile video shops, it was the mobile food store which, to varying degrees, remained an important lifeline for such non-mobile people in all areas.

Schools

Across the four study areas a higher proportion of respondents reported an improvement in school services (16.9 per cent, compared with 7.4 per cent who perceived a deterioration). Expressions of improvement were greatest in the Teifi Valley (24.1 per cent) and Betws-y-coed (18.0 per cent) study areas, whilst more than one-tenth of respondents in the Tanat Valley and Devil's Bridge areas had noted a deterioration in school services over recent years.

An often-repeated belief regarding the continuation of the 'living' village is the importance of the existence of the village school. It is uncertain to what degree this is 'received wisdom', or is a fair comment based on expressed experience in rural areas. Certainly rural education provision continues to attract attention, particularly regarding the potential conflict of economic and social rationales for school maintenance (Robinson, 1990). However, as Lievesley and Maynard (1992) observe, attention is almost always focused on primary school provision, with much less concern being voiced over junior and secondary schools. It is possible that the experience of travelling some distance to schools for 11+ education is so commonplace that it does not occur as a matter of concern in rural service debates. However, we found that across rural Wales, an average of 41.1 per cent of respondents reported problems faced by their child(ren) in travelling to school.

We would suggest that there is a need for further research on these matters, as the questionnaire from which this survey is derived could not and did not approach the wider questions of the values invested in local education provision. However, some qualitative comment, both from the questionnaires and from interviews in the study areas, suggests that there is an importance attached to rural schools that is beyond basic quantification.

> The youngsters go away to college and work, and there is no one to carry on the traditions. Once us old ones die off there'll be no one. (2194, Devil's Bridge)

> To me [community] would mean social intercourse – knowing each other, kids at school together. (4138, Teifi Valley)

We also asked about the existence and need for pre-school provision. Although few people reported the existence of pre-school facilities, our survey revealed considerable expressed interest concerning increased provision of such facilities. Most interest appeared to be in getting pre-school children to mix and thus broaden their social experience (the average over the four study areas was 35.7 per cent, with 'getting children used to school' as the second most popular response at 26.4 per cent). A further 21.4 per cent of respondents cited 'building up friendships in the community' and 10.7 per cent stated that increased provision would give 'mothers their own time'. Indeed, building up friendships in the community was the most popular reason given in Betws-y-coed, and the second most popular in Devil's Bridge, which indicates something important about people's broader experiences of community involvement and engagement – or perhaps the lack of it.

Despite this, the majority of answers were reasoned from the point of view of what was best for children, rather than as allowing parents free time or as a community meeting place. It is difficult to state with any certainty that this was genuinely felt, or whether admitting that pre-school groups benefit people other than children is felt to be an abdication of parental responsibility. Certainly, the lack of out-of-home pre-school activity can severely restrict opportunities for the 'carer' parent/guardian (usually the mother), thus contributing to her, and the child(ren)'s, isolation from alternative opportunities or social milieux. In rural areas the lack of pre-school facilities may emphasize isolation, as there are very few sites where those with pre-school-age children can meet, which may in turn lead to a house-based lifestyle with little social interaction.

One common criticism of rural lifestyles is the relative lack of out-of-school facilities for children. Our responses showed that such activities were available for many children, with an average participation across all study areas of 56.8 per cent.

Most reported activities were in Betws-y-coed at 71.4 per cent and least in the Teifi Valley at 42.5 per cent, again emphasizing the variability and differences between rural areas. Given the variable location of these activities, access to private transport would still seem to have been of considerable importance, even though many activities did take place in the same village as the respondent's residence (ranging from 68.8 per cent in Betws-y-coed to 25.0 per cent in the Teifi Valley). Most, however (an average across the four study areas of 59.6 per cent), occurred outside the village. The Tanat Valley had 31.6 per cent reported as in the next village, and 47.8 per cent of Devil's Bridge respondents reported such activities as taking place in the nearest town (presumably Aberystwyth). In these instances, access to private or public transport was essential. Public transport frequently did not often run outside school hours, thus compounding this difficulty (see also Moyes, 1989, who cites travel to after-school activities as one of the major instances of unmet need in terms of public transport provision in rural Wales).

Health

Health services, much like schools, are accorded greater personal significance than are many other services such as shops, for example. Across the four study areas 25.9 per cent of respondents reported improvements in health services over the past five years, a much higher proportion than the 7.0 per cent reporting a deterioration. The highest perceived rate of improvement was witnessed in the Tanat Valley (43.3 per cent) – a level double that recorded in each of the other three study areas – and deterioration in health services was reported most frequently in the Teifi Valley. Again, it must be stressed that a majority of respondents in each study area reported that they were unaware of changes within such provision over recent years. Although the five-year period preceding our survey post-dated the harsher rationalizations of local health services, it pre-dated recent reforms such as the introduction of fund-holding general practices and NHS trusts. It would seem fair to suggest that the situation regarding health service provision in rural areas needs to be carefully monitored in the wake of these recent reforms, so that rural residents – particularly non-mobile and low-income groups – do not become a hidden health problem.

Our surveys yielded interesting and detailed information about health-related problems in our study areas. The percentage of adults who reported having experienced serious (long-term) health problems ranged from 49.0 per cent in the Teifi Valley to 29.0 per cent of residents in the Betws-y-coed study area. Interestingly there was no clear correlation between the age structure of the sample population and the level of serious health problems. Indeed, Betws-y-coed contained the highest proportion of residents aged over sixty-five years and the lowest proportion of reported serious health problems. Although it is not easy to offer explanations for this geographical variation, it is worth noting that the average incidence of serious health problems across rural Wales (44.0 per cent) was at a much higher rate than that recorded in the 1991 Census for Wales as a whole (17.1 per cent of all persons).

We find it difficult to put forward any definitive reasoning for the disparity between the reported ill-health levels in Betws-y-coed and the other areas of rural Wales. Rather, it is probable that there is a complex relationship of influences that include, for example, wealth and income levels, the perception of retirement (as a positive or negative attribute of lifestyle), choice of living location (whether of necessity, or more individually proactive) and the consequences of life in a remote or pressured rural area according to personal aspirations (for a fuller social life or for 'peace and quiet'). However, it should be noted that a majority of respondents within each Welsh study area reported no serious health problems – although the level of 44 per cent who did gives some cause for concern.

We also asked about the number of visits to the doctors and to hospitals for the first two people in the household. The responses seem to suggest that although serious health problems exhibit a particular geographical distribution, this did not appear to be related to either minor health problems or the decision to visit the doctor about these, although Betws-y-coed contained the highest proportion of persons who had not visited the doctor (41.4 per cent) and the highest proportion who had not visited a hospital (96.4 per cent) in the previous twelve months. By contrast, three-quarters of persons living in the Devil's Bridge and Teifi Valley study areas had visited the doctor over the past year – an extremely high percentage.

Generally the level of satisfaction with health services appeared high, with a large majority of respondents reporting that they were either very satisfied or quite satisfied with health services in their area. In each study area the level of satisfaction was in excess of 75 per cent, and ranged from 77.5 per cent in Betws-y-coed to 89.6 per cent in the Tanat Valley. We asked an indirect question about satisfaction with the health service by recording the percentage of people (first two in household) who had used private health-care facilities in the previous twelve months. Across the four Welsh study areas, only 3.0 per cent of persons reported using private medical facilities in the previous twelve months, with highest use recorded in the Devil's Bridge area (6.4 per cent) and lowest in Betws-y-coed (0.6 per cent). It appears, then, that private medical treatment was used by relatively fewer people in our study areas, which again confirms the view of Bell and Cloke (1989) that there are significant difficulties involved in introducing privatized services into sparsely populated rural areas.

These issues of ill-health and health care are closely intercon-nected with the wider theme of accessibility that has formed the focus of this chapter. Certainly issues of physical isolation and health were often interconnected in our respondents' experiences of rural lifestyles. Our research showed a very heavy reliance on private cars for getting to hospital, varying from 69.2 per cent in Betws-y-coed to 52.3 per cent in the Devil's Bridge area. There was a high figure for ambulance use in Devil's Bridge (37.0 per cent) and the Tanat Valley (35.1 per cent), whilst 7.7 per cent relied on a hired car or taxi in Betws-y-coed.

As with other issues of accessibility and isolation, it would appear from our questionnaire that the experience of isolation from health services was influenced by gender, with women in three of our four study areas experiencing relatively greater difficulties than men in this respect. Only in the Devil's Bridge area did more men than women report difficulties reaching a doctor/health service. We also asked people's opinion on whether rural areas could manage with fewer health services than their urban counterparts. The overwhelming conclusion to be drawn here is that the majority of respondents in each area (the least was in Devil's Bridge at 72.2 per cent) did not feel rural areas could manage with fewer health services than urban areas. When qualified, the reasons were often those of equity with other areas, and of the impositions of providing health care over a large area with low population density.

> Out in the sticks with no hospital immediately on hand there should be more medical services if anything. (3187, Tanat Valley)

> Population more sparse, difficult to get to services. We're entitled to as good a service as in town. (4063, Teifi Valley)

> I think rural areas need more medical services because it's harder to reach services in the countryside than in the town. (1222, Betws-y-coed)

> People need more [health care] in the country because people are more dispersed and have more difficulty getting to places to be treated. (2093, Devil's Bridge)

These replies suggest that, perhaps of all the aspects of accessibility covered in this chapter, it is the question of access to increasingly centralized health services which is the most important for policy-makers to bear in mind over future years. Despite the impression that the countryside is now populated by two-car-owning households, there remain significant non-mobile groups who in some locations cannot make easy journeys to GPs or to hospital. It will be crucial to ensure that through dedicated transport services (e.g. ambulances), through maintained public transport services or through *comprehensive* coverage of community-based transport schemes, these 'hidden' non-mobile groups in the rural population can continue to use the public health-care service.

Conclusions

At the beginning of this chapter we raised a number of questions about what are commonly conceived of as rural accessibility problems. These concerned both the transport links available to rural people and the services to which they require such links. Clearly the high levels of vehicle ownership, including what appeared to be some reluctant car ownership, in rural areas were both a response to the accessibility conditions prevailing in the countryside, and a hindrance to any form of commercially viable system of public transport. Our research has offered further evidence, however, that access to private transport was highly differentiated both within and between households, with age, gender and low income being important contributory factors to non-mobility in this respect. Accordingly, there appeared to be significant minorities of people in rural areas who were non-mobile and were, therefore, dependent on bus services or lifts to gain access to facilities and services that were not available *in situ*. As with the incidence of low-income households (chapter 6), these groups were not disappearing from villages, but appear to have been reproduced through processes of in-migration or ageing (or both).

Perhaps more surprisingly, our respondents saw a mix of deterioration and improvement in their local services. Public transport, shops and post offices were on balance seen as having deteriorated, whereas local education and health services were on balance thought to have improved. New rural residents appeared to have accepted and become accustomed to low-level service environments, and often had the personal mobility to gain relatively easy access to services that were urban-based. Without having lived through the history of rural service rationalization, newer residents seemed to have relatively lower expectations of services than residents who had lived through the period of service closures. In this context, any improvements to the quality of services in the five years prior to our survey might have contributed to an overall perception of improved service infrastructure.

Although subsidies for transport to schools had not yet been seriously eroded and, therefore, access to education was not a major issue for our respondents, significant changes have taken place in shopping habits, and serious fears were being expressed about the quality of, and access to, health-care services. Despite the fact that an important minority of rural people continued to use local shops for their everyday shopping needs, there seemed to be an inexorable increase in the use of (sub)urban-based supermarkets. This suggests not only patterns of shopping behaviour on the grounds of cost, choice and convenience, but also that the culturally symbolic place of the local shop at the heart of the village may have been eroding in some places. Again it was the non-mobile groups in rural areas who made most essential use of village shops and post offices, and who would be most jeopardized by their potential demise. And it was these same groups who were finding it increasingly inconvenient and difficult to gain access to urban-based medical services.

The increasingly common assumption of countryside people as two-car-owning meritocracies (for whom the effort of making their own way to centralized services was a small price to pay for the environmental delights of rural living) can only serve to hide, in increasing measure, the plight of the non-mobile minority in gaining access to basic and necessary lifestyle opportunities. Interestingly, although accessibility is the conventional heading under which to discuss the problems encountered by rural people living 'away from it all', many of our respondents tended to refer instead to the more all-embracing notion of isolation. In so doing they made a number of connections between the problems experienced in overcoming geographical isolation due to the lack of public transport, and in some cases lack of private mobility, and the different experiences of coping with the social and psychological isolation which can arise in a rural environment. Depending on these connections, such isolation is a dream come true for some, an incarceration for others and perhaps a mix of the two for most. These varying ideas and experiences of rural living are the subject of chapter 7.

References

Action with Communities in Rural England (1992) *Annual Report,* ACRE, Cirencester.

Association of County Councils (1979) *Rural Deprivation,* ACC, London.

Association of District Councils (1978) *Rural Recovery: Strategy for Survival,* ADC, London.

Banister, D. (1980) *Transport, Mobility and Deprivation in Inter-urban Areas*, Saxon House, Farnborough.

Bell, P., and Cloke, P. (1989) 'The changing relationship between the private and public sectors: privatisation and rural Britain', *Journal of Rural Studies*, 5, 1–15.

Bell, P. and Cloke, P. (1990) 'Bus deregulation and rural localities: an example from Wales', in P. Bell and P. Cloke (eds.), *Deregulation and Transport: Market Forces in the Modern World*, David Fulton, London.

Bell, P., and Cloke, P. (1991) 'Deregulation and rural bus services: a study in rural Wales', *Environment and Planning A*, 23, 107–26.

Blackaby, D., Murphy, P., O'Leary, N. and Thomas, E. (1995) 'Wales: an economic survey', *Contemporary Wales*, 8, 213–95.

Clark, D. and Woollett, S. (1990) *English Village Services in the Eighties*, Rural Development Commission, London.

Cloke, P. (1979) *Key Settlements in Rural Areas*, Methuen, London.

Cloke, P. (1983) *An Introduction to Rural Settlement Planning*, Methuen, London.

Cloke, P. (1984) 'Traditional wisdoms in rural transport and accessibility', in P. Cloke (ed.), *Wheels within Wales*, Centre for Rural Transport, Lampeter.

Cloke, P. (1986) 'Accessibility and service planning' in P. Lowe, T. Bradley and S. Wright (eds.), *Deprivation and Welfare in Rural Areas*, Geobooks, Norwich.

Clout, H. (1972) *An Introduction to Rural Geography*, Pergamon, London.

Central Statistical Office (1992) *Social Trends, 1992*, HMSO, London.

Lievesley, K. and Maynard, W. (1992) *1991 Survey of Rural Services*, Rural Development Commission, London.

Moseley, M. J. (1979) *Accessibility: The Rural Challenge*, Methuen, London.

Moyes, T. (1989) *The Need for Public Transport in Mid-Wales: Normative Approaches and their Implications*, Rural Surveys Research Unit, Aberystwyth.

Nutley, S. (1982) 'The extent of public transport decline in rural Wales', *Cambria*, 9, 27–48.

Nutley, S. (1983) *Transport Policy Appraisal and Personal Accessibility in Rural Wales*, Geobooks, Norwich.

Nutley, S. (1984) 'Accessibility issues in rural Wales', in P. Cloke (ed.), *Wheels within Wales*, Centre for Rural Transport, Lampeter.

Office of Population and Census Suveys (1992) *U.K. Census 1991*, OPCS, London.

Robinson, G. M. (1990) *Conflict and Change in the Countryside*, Belhaven, London.

Shaw, M. (1979) 'Rural deprivation and social planning: an overview', in M. Shaw (ed.), *Rural Deprivation and Planning*, Geobooks, Norwich.

Standing Conference of Rural Community Councils (1978) *The Decline in Rural Services*, NCSS, London.

6 • Experiencing Low Income and Poverty in Rural Wales

Introduction

> The isolated rural communities are, of themselves, poor in material resources, and their efforts have, therefore, not until recently gone into great buildings or sculpture or painting or orchestral music ... Rather they have found their scope in poetry and oratory and song, arts in which the poorest labourer can often compete with his richer neighbours. In this way, and in others as well, poverty has been a safeguard of that intensely democratic feeling which is such a feature of modern Wales as well as a help towards the survival of the language and its associations. (Fleure, 1941, xiv)

In this chapter, we discuss the findings of our Rural Lifestyles surveys in relation to the levels of income and poverty existing in our four study areas in rural Wales. This is not a straightforward task, for a number of reasons. As Fleure notes in this foreword to Bowen's classic 1941 book on *Wales: A Study of Geography and History*, the more isolated rural communities of Wales have traditionally been regarded as synonymous with poverty. Yet, in combination with this recognition that poverty exists, comes the acknowledgement that there are important interconnections between these 'impoverished' lifestyles and the preservation of an essential democracy and a living indigenous culture. Well into the second half of the twentieth century, these links have been emphasized between what some would see as the 'disadvantages' of rural living, and the very definite advantages of focusing on the cultures of mind and spirit rather than on those of materialism. E. G. Bowen (1957) for example, in his essay on the rural 'Heartland' of Wales, notes that

> In these areas and under these conditions, the cultural life of the people remains more closely associated with the things of the mind and the spirit ... than is the case in the more populous and sophisticated areas on the lowlands. (pp.280–1)

This notion that the evils of poverty and an 'unsophisticated' lifestyle in rural Wales are entwined with the glories of cultural distinction and psychological 'income', provides an essential back-cloth to this chapter.

However, as we have discussed elsewhere in this book, the demographic shifts of the 1970s and 1980s have served to muddy what were hithertofore perceived as deep and clear-running waters. By 1977, David Thomas was noting a 'swiftly changing countryside and people' in rural Wales (p.8). The in-migration of new rural dwellers, many English, some elderly, and others pursuing a wide range of 'alternative' lifestyles, not only introduced different forms of potential and actual impoverishment into the Welsh countryside, but it also placed indigenous poverty into a different context. Assumptions which equated rural disadvantage in Wales with the spiritually and culturally fulfilled life of a farm labourer, cannot easily be stretched to encompass the stranded English retiree, the struggling self-employed escapee from the English urban rat race, or the often basic life of the new-age traveller. Such people may well be experiencing low income and poverty, but their presence in rural Wales forms part of the in-migratory challenge to the cultural distinction and associated values of traditional Welsh rural life. In-migrants bring with them different mental images and ideas about what rural life is like – still perhaps focusing on the things of the mind and the spirit, but usually responding to very different cultural norms and expectations. These new rural poverties challenge the 'democratic feeling' expressed in Fleure's 1941 account, and may be regarded as part of the sweeping flood-tide which threatens the very survival of 'language and its associations' which he regarded as being upheld by poverty in its traditional form.

The counter-urbanizing movement of English migrants into rural Wales has also muddied the waters of policy responses to rural disadvantage. As Clare Wenger (1980) so powerfully demonstrated, the combination of population decline, economic marginality and lack of growth permitted a very clear identification of mid-Wales as 'a region of rural deprivation' (p.2). Accordingly, the amelioration of these conditions was sought through the Development of Rural Wales Act 1976, establishing a Development Board charged with the mission of facilitating economic growth (and by implication, rising living standards) in rural Wales. However, with in-migration has come something of a cultural change in the broad-sweep appreciation of rural issues. The very English notion that the countryside is a repository of affluence, and that movement into rural areas implies a further infusion of moneyed classes, has to some extent been attached culturally to rural Wales. After all, if so many people are freely choosing to establish a lifestyle in rural Wales, then some would want to claim that living standards must have become, or perhaps have always been, more acceptable than was suggested by descriptions of mid-Wales as a region of deprivation. Any such allegations are, of course, an invidious over-simplification of the complexities of rural life. However, we now live in an age of the rolling-back of the welfare state, and the favouring of market mechanisms. In this context it is perhaps easy to see that individual decisions to move into rural Wales will collec-tively suggest a gloss of increasing affluence which, as in rural England, tends to cover over problems and concerns in rural communities.

To paint a picture of the experience of low income and poverty in 1990s rural Wales, then, requires some careful consideration of what we mean by such terms as deprivation, disadvantage and poverty, and of how such conditions are interconnected with the cultural constructs of rurality which influence expectations, norms and even policy responses.

Cultures of poverty? The 'deprivation' debate

Until recently, the term 'deprivation' has been widely adopted as a focus for describing and explaining the problems of rural life. We have suggested elsewhere (Cloke et al., 1995a) that the early use of this term was very probably associated with highly defensible polit-ical motives relating to the objective of highlighting some of the inequalities occurring in rural areas owing to wider processes of economic restructuring, social recomposition and the rationalization of state-sector interventions in housing, service and employment markets. Although the existence of 'haves' and 'have-nots' in rural areas has been clearly visible, if often mythologized, throughout rural history (Mingay 1989a, b, c), rural researchers have used the notion of deprivation to suggest that the rapid socio-economic changes of the 1970s and 1980s acted to 'deprive' certain sections of the population of key opportunities and resources which were judged as necessary for acceptable living standards in rural areas.

In this way, the term 'deprivation' became loaded with a number of questionable assumptions:

> Who is to judge what is 'acceptable'? Is it legitimate in the identification of 'depriving' processes of change to transfer the stigmatic label of 'deprived' to places, and more importantly to people? Is it more important to publicise rural problems of deprivation than to accept the accounts of the people concerned as to whether or not they recognised themselves as deprived? Is the conceptual distance between poverty and deprivation such that 'deprivation' is automatically corrupted in discursive terms in that it is accepting of the state's subterfuge regarding the non-existence of poverty? Would the concept of deprivation itself become limited by its nominal acceptance by particular decision-making interest groups in rural areas? (Cloke et al., 1995, 352)

With hindsight, these assumptions restrict the conceptual power of the idea of deprivation. In the 1970s and 1980s, however, rural researchers were principally concerned with an evaluation of socio-economic change, and of policy-making responses to such change. For example, the seminal collections by Shaw (1979) and Walker (1978) stemmed from conferences designed to publicize the hidden nature of rural problems. Shaw's emphasis on 'deprivation' emerged from the research community of local authority planners, and reflected a political concern for the spatial issues of change and its impacts on rural communities. Walker's emphasis on 'poverty' was embedded in the disciplinary discourses of social policy, and in the political pressure exerted by the Child Poverty Action Group. The concept of poverty permitted the emphasis on rural problems as an outcome of social structuring. Such problems were experienced by individuals and class-related groups, and could be addressed through welfare provision to individuals and households. Shaw's deprivation approach, however, emphasized the role of planners and policy-makers in the provision of key opportunities in the places where they were needed.

Until recently it has been Shaw's approach which has found favour in both academic and policy-making discourse on rural issues. He suggested three categories of deprivation which combine in a self-sustaining spiral of disadvantage: household deprivation, opportunity deprivation and mobility deprivation (see chapter 4, pp.77–9).

Shaw's typology has subsequently been criticized because of its emphasis on space rather than society, and because it permitted the debate on rural problems to be conflated with debates over resource allocations to rural local authorities (see Bradley et al., 1986; McLaughlin, 1986; Cloke et al., 1995b). Nevertheless, deprivation was used as the focus of the only major research study of rural problems in Britain (and for Britain here read England) during the 1980s. McLaughlin's (1985) study of five case-study areas in rural England was financed by the Department of the Environment, and consisted of lengthy household surveys which yielded considerable information under the headings suggested by Shaw to be components of deprivation. Despite this breadth of information, one particular set of findings came to symbolize McLaughlin's study. He generated an index of households in each study area based on annual gross disposable income expressed as a percentage of supplementary benefit levels plus actual housing costs. Drawing on a methodology developed by Townsend (1975, 1979) he defined a threshold of 139 per cent as being in or near the margins of poverty, and concluded that the following levels of 'poverty' existed in each area:

Essex	24.9 per cent
Northumberland	27.3 per cent
Shropshire	24.9 per cent
Suffolk	21.4 per cent
Yorkshire	25.8 per cent

This set of findings caught the collective imaginations of many researchers and policy-makers interested in rural problems, and ever since, these figures have been used to illustrate the existence of 'deprivation' in rural areas. For example, the report of the Archbishop's Commission on Rural Areas (1990), *Faith In The Countryside,* suggested:

> We are convinced by the argument in the report to the Department of the Environment by McLaughlin (1985), which indicated that approximately 25% of households in rural areas were living in or on the margins of poverty ... we would suggest that since that survey was undertaken, the degree of relative deprivation in rural areas may well have increased. (pp.92–3)

One important aspect of the McLaughlin study and its aftermath is that a specific measure of relative income, labelled as indicating whether a household was 'in or on the margins of poverty' became equated with 'relative deprivation'. This quite understandable elision of very different conceptual ideas about problems has served to obscure the meaning of each. So while deprivation has become a convenient metaphor for the most pressing problems in rural areas (Cloke, 1993, 1995) the meanings attributable to that metaphor are contemporaneously 'known' yet 'obscured'. As we suggest elsewhere, deprivation thus has a double twist,

> at once giving lip service to some notion of problems in rural life, and offering a political shrug of the shoulders about the difficulties of doing anything about it. The inheritance to rural studies in Britain of the concept of deprivation is a 'curious doublethink' (Roberts, 1992) whereby the idea that rural areas experience the same kind of social disruption and problems as do inner cities is strongly contested, yet policy agencies and other establishment interests continue to identify social disruption and problems in the rural context. (Cloke et al., 1995, 353)

We would further suggest that the use of the deprivation metaphor in rural Wales, especially in relation to the work of local authorities and the Development Board for Rural Wales, will inevitably have encountered this same doublethink. Many of those actors in public decision-making processes associated with rural Wales have found themselves having to make use of the concept of deprivation because of its place in wider policy discourses, but concomitantly have found that by speaking of deprivation they have had to take on conceptual baggage which is bound up with debates between the English central and local states and which reflects the English governmental position of acknowledging 'deprivation', but only in such a way as to minimize the imperative for policy response.

Cultures of poverty? Rurality and 'idyllization'

In order further to unpack this 'curious doublethink' which is integral to the metaphor of deprivation, we suggest that it is useful to attempt to reclaim some strands of poverty studies in rural research. In so doing, we readily acknowledge the parallel difficulties in reaching unambiguous conceptualizations of poverty. As Mingione (1993) suggests,

> Poverty is a difficult question from both a methodological and a theoretical point of view. Furthermore, it is a very ambiguous political issue. Many difficulties derive from the irreducible distance between the abstract concept and the findings of research. The concept is based on the idea that, for various reasons and for variable periods of time, a part of the population lacks access to sufficient resources to enable it to survive at a historically or geographically determined minimum standard of life, and that this leads to serious consequences in terms of behaviour and social relations. (p.324)

Thus, little consensus exists on any standard definition or measurement of poverty, and therefore the use of the concept of poverty in rural areas seems little different from that of deprivation in terms of our ability to illuminate the obscure (Milbourne, 1996). However, it is interesting that a number of authors have sought to interconnect social geographies of life within the 'rural idyll' with the idea that poverty in rural areas is somehow being hidden or rejected *culturally* both by rural residents (some of whom might be labelled 'deprived' or 'poor' by normative approaches to the issue, such as that employed by McLaughlin) and by the decision-makers with jurisdiction over rural areas.

Most of these attempts at interconnection have been centred on cultural ideas of village *England*, but we discuss them here partly because constructions of Welsh rural culture will also, we suggest, be intertwined with popular discourses about rural poverty, and partly because *English* rural idylls are being diffused into rural Wales in the packing cases of English in-migrants. An illustration of some of these important links is provided by Bradley et al. (1986), who have described how rural deprivation has been wrapped up with ideological rhetoric about village England, with the result that the environmental appeal of a conserved countryside and its settlements has precluded a proper understanding of social problems experienced by rural people:

> Rural mythology thus complements many of the wide-spread and basic racial, ethnic and cultural prejudices which lie at the heart of attitudes concerning poverty in the UK. One set of prejudices reinforces another, such that 'village 'England' ideology is a force for negative discrimination

against the poor and deprived, whether they live in urban or rural areas. For on the one side it denies citizenship to the urban poor, and on the other refuses even to acknowledge the existence of poverty in rural areas . . . indeed to admit the existence of poverty (and deprivation based on inequalities between people, rather than places) in rural areas is to challenge one of the most pervasive images of our social heritage. (p.25)

Both in rural areas, and beyond, cultural constructions of rurality which (re)produce and (re)negotiate arcadian and pastoral idylls about rural life might therefore be thought to exert a pervasive yet obfuscatory influence over the recognition of poverty in rural areas. By this token rural people might be thought of as 'deprived' in relation to the facilities and opportunities of urban life, but they cannot be viewed as impoverished because of the perceived compensation inherent in rural life and the lower expectations which follow. The poor can thus be disregarded as being 'content' with their (undemanding) rural life, and the not-so-poor will not be able to reconcile the idea of poverty with the idyllized imagined geographies of the village, so that any material evidence of poverty will be screened out culturally. Such an effect is exacerbated if, for example, it can be suggested that a simple and non-materialistic lifestyle needs to be maintained as a bastion against modernistic tendencies which threaten particular cultural attributes of traditional rural idylls. If Fleure's association of poverty with the idea of safeguarding both traditionally 'intense democratic feelings' and the 'survival of the (Welsh) language and its associations' is to be taken at face value, then there may be particular forms of the hiddenness of deprivation and poverty in rural Wales.

Clearly the English rural idyll conjures up a different mix of cultural histories, geographies, practices and expectations from that likely to be encountered in any equivalent Welsh idyll. Some aspects may overlap, particularly as Welsh rural life is overlaid by successive layers of in-migration from England, but we suggest later in this chapter that cultural constructs of Welsh rurality can in many ways be distinctive (see Cloke and Davies, 1992; Cloke and Milbourne, 1992). Nevertheless, it is possible in a more general sense for us to suggest that mythical values of rural idyll do underpin attitudes to rural poverty. In a study of poverty in rural Leicestershire, Fabes et al. (1983) suggest two such underpinnings. First,

The rural idyll exacerbates poverty by maintaining rural deprivation because it is that very deprivation – lack of housing, transport, employment opportunities – which makes an area rural and so attractive to the urban dweller. (p.54)

Secondly,

The rural idyll conceals poverty. In this respect, the poor unwittingly conspire with the more affluent to hide their own poverty by denying its existence. Those values which are at the heart of the rural idyll result in the poor tolerating their material deprivation because of the priority given to those symbols of the rural idyll: the family, the work ethic and good health. And when that material deprivation becomes so chronic by the standard of the area that it has to be recognised by the poor themselves, shame forces secrecy and the management of that poverty within the smallest possible framework . . . the newcomers do not want to see poverty because it is anathema to the rural idyll which they are seeking to preserve . . . newcomers because of their perceptions of their own status and that of indigenous working class, have taken over the paternalistic role of the traditional land-owning class. (pp.55–66)

In twenty intensive interviews with households which, using normative poverty indicators, would be regarded as in poverty, Fabes et al. identify strongly differentiated attitudes towards people's own poverty. These included a fatalistic acceptance of a lowly position within a clearly perceived social hierarchy; a high tolerance of poverty, making do for as long as possible without taking action; a lack of material aspirations, emphasizing instead the importance of health, family and cultural heritage; and elements of shame and secrecy, recognizing the stigmatic problems of seeking advice or help. Such responses suggest that the experience of poverty is multifaceted and easily caricatured as low expectations compensated by the positive aspects of rural life. As Scott et al. (1991) insist:

People don't seem to 'put up with' service deficiencies because other parts of their life are good. 'Low' expectations is perhaps better expressed as 'different' expectations, normal, and in the main accepted; almost approved by dint of their midwife role to self-sufficiency and 'learning to make do'. Life is a whole experience. (p.51)

We believe that these two suggestions – that rural idyll exacerbates poverty, and that rural idyll conceals poverty – need to be carefully placed in particular contexts. As we suggest in chapter 7, the forms and practices of rural community that we discovered in our interviews in rural Wales certainly do not conform to any English idyll. Neither are notions of settlement, aesthetics, nature–society relations and, particularly, nationalism transferable from one context to the other. Nevertheless, we remain convinced that a form of culturally constructed rurality exists in Wales which is able both to exacerbate and to conceal poverty. Moreover, there is a further interconnection between rural cultures and poverty which is constructed at a more discursive level. Cloke (1995) has argued that the discursive transformation of poverty in Britain during the Thatcher years has had a peculiarly rural component. The broadly 'idyllized' construction of rural areas as happy, healthy, self-supporting and close to nature has permitted a political interpretation that these are problem-free areas. Moreover, rurality has been characterized as the acceptable 'other' to constructions of the urban which are characterized by crime, pollution, the 'undeserving' poor and so on. Rural areas have thus become a kind of repository for late-twentieth-century (English) national values. In addition to the traditional values as the heartland of the (English) nation (Matless, 1994) rural areas can now be used to demonstrate the perfection of a society and an economy which has been transformed by the release of market forces by political programmes of privatization and deregulation. Rurality *is* self-help and self-support; it is becoming the non-interventionist arena where capitalist processes permit 'ideal' lives; it is where Thatcherite political values can be demonstrated spatially.

The degree to which this spatial demonstration effect applies specifically to rural Wales is arguable. The operations of the Development Board for Rural Wales and the Welsh Development Agency might suggest that the particular spatial effects of the Thatcherite transformation have been ameliorated in rural Wales (as in rural Scotland) because of the presence and activities of particular policy-making agencies with rural jurisdictions. However, given the marked shift in the strategic nature of these development agencies in rural Wales, from a culture of interventionist development to a culture of training and enterprise facilitation, many would argue that the colonial hand of the Whitehall-based state remains enormously influential over policy affairs in Wales. Thereby we again have to conclude that some of the Englishness of rural and policy discourses does seem to rub off in the contexts of rural Wales.

These interconnections between deprivation, poverty and cultures of rurality have significant implications for research on the subject of the essential problems of rural life. We have suggested that 'deprivation' represents a very interesting metaphorical device which allows at one and the same time the *recognition* of forms of inequality in rural areas and the *disenfranchisement* of these inequalities from major political and policy response, on the grounds that rural needs are different from elsewhere. The seemingly all-powerful acceptance of this metaphor in policy-making and academic discourses is upheld by the cultural acceptance of imagined rural lifestyles which are in various ways 'idyllized'. This occurs at various scales of discourse and at various scales of response to material conditions and change. It is implicated in national levels of discursive transformations of poverty, in the assumed scope for action and professional assumptions found in national, regional and local levels of decision-making agencies, in the practices by which poverty is hidden from or filtered out by, affluent rural residents, and in the self-reflections of the rural poor themselves. For these and other reasons, research which focuses on issues of deprivation and poverty needs to be sensitive to the evident difficulties which are inherent in attaching precise meanings to the metaphor of deprivation.

Deprivation: the context of rural Wales

> The Welsh concept of community owes much to the relationship between people and the environment in which they live ... Any discussion on countryside policy must, in my view, begin by acknowledging the need for local communities to exercise real influence over their lives, and the way our planning, economic and transport policies are shaped. (Wyn Jones, 1991, 41)

It is clear that rural Wales represents a particular ethnic and cultural context within the wider notion of rural Britain. With an indigenous and living language and associated social, cultural and political organizations, as well as the deeply rooted community ethic based on like-speaking kith and kin, rural Wales has a distinctive

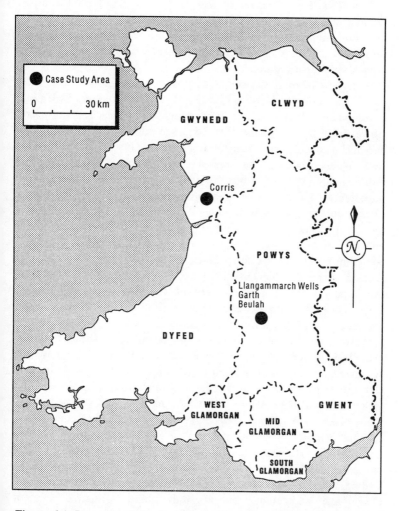

Figure 6.1: Location of the Corris and Llangammarch study areas

assemblage of social relations which cannot easily be conflated with parallel ideas of English rural idyll, or with the cultural contests occurring in rural England between 'locals' and 'newcomers'. If 'deprivation' is to be seen as a normative measure of how economic restructuring and social recomposition 'deprive' certain individuals and households of opportunities, and if 'poverty' refers to the experienced lack of resources that reduces standards of life below relative minima, and has serious consequences for social relations, then both deprivation and poverty will in turn be intertwined in rural Wales with a series of traditions and aspirations relating to aspects of Welsh culture.

It is well beyond the scope of this book to present a detailed account of modern Welsh political and cultural identity, its historic development, or the image with which it approaches its future. However it is undeniable that language lies at the core of both personal and corporate constructions of rurality in large tracts of rural Wales, and that the implication of Welshness(es) for understanding issues of deprivation and poverty is paramount. The importance of these issues was highlighted very clearly in a study carried out by Cloke and Davies (1992) which in some ways was a precursor to the Rural Lifestyles research in Wales. The study focused on two very different areas of rural Wales – Corris, a community in a Welsh-speaking area of north Wales, and Llangammarch Wells/Garth/Beulah, a collection of settlements in the largely English-speaking area of the Welsh borders (Figure 6.1). It was designed to gain some preliminary information about the nature of deprivation in two contrasting communities, where language and cultural practice were expected to be markedly different. Sixty households were interviewed in each area, and the overall results are summarized in Figures 6.2 and 6.3. The strong impression presented by these findings is that one community, Corris, did appear to be a place where deprivation existed, and was commonly recognized as such by its residents, whereas the other community, Llangammarch, appeared to be a place where deprivation was less of a problem. However, a replication of McLaughlin's (1986) index of those households in or on the margins of poverty resulted in the finding that, at 30.6 per cent and 29.0 per cent respectively, the Corris and Llangammarch areas did exhibit normative signs of deprivation which were higher than those found in his five English case studies.

A closer examination of qualitative evidence from these interviews suggested that in Corris there was a conjoining of social divisions within the community with a very strong sense of the *loss* of cultural integrity within that community. Even though Welsh-speaking social and educational institutions had not become Anglicized, and some of the non-Welsh in-migrants had made

Figure 6.2: Corris

Corris is located at the south-east extremity of Gwynedd and is bound up with particular rounds of socio-economic change. Ten slate quarries once operated in the area, but only one remains, and the diminishing agricultural and forestry sectors have also left vacuums in the traditional economic *raison d'être* of the community. There have been significant social and cultural changes in the post-war period, particularly relating to the diminution and dilution of the local 'culture' and the Welsh language due to the in-migration of English-speakers both as full-time residents and as holiday-home owners. The main problems perceived by residents are:

- A lack of rented housing and the inflated price of owner-occupied housing, which make it difficult for young people to stay in the area.
- The distances travelled to gain employment, accessibility to those workplaces, and the lack of training opportunities for young people.
- Low incomes – nearly 50% of respondents received a net income of less than £9,000 per year.
- The deregulation of bus services in 1985 was perceived to have caused some disruption to local services.
- Most respondents felt that there had been a loss of community locally and felt disadvantaged because of a lack of social facilities.

In all, 63 per cent of respondents in Corris thought that deprivation and disadvantage existed in rural areas, and the survey did seem to point to some familiar elements of rural deprivation. The problem of low income was experienced particularly by Welsh-speaking families, as was a general shortage of well-paid jobs within reasonable travelling distance. The cumulative impact of holiday homes, holiday cottages for limited let, and the shortage of building land made it difficult for young people and the elderly to gain access to appropriate housing. Again, Welsh-speaking households were worst affected, but some young English households experienced equal difficulties. Problems of poor public transport and lack of mobility compounded the lifestyle difficulties experienced by elderly Welsh low-income groups. Having to rely on village shops or mobile shops added to the drain on their already meagre financial resources. Information from Corris therefore suggests severe problems of cumulative rural deprivation experienced chiefly by low-income and non-mobile groups in the community.

Source: Cloke and Davies (1992).

Figure 6.3: Llangammarch Wells/Garth/Beulah

These communities are situated some 8–10 miles west of Builth Wells in Powys. There is no significant history here of industrial activity apart from primary rural production, and over recent years the area has undergone a steady recomposition, with older (often retired) people moving in to replace younger local people who have moved away to seek better employment opportunities. The main problems perceived by residents are:

• The difficulties encountered by local young households in finding suitable housing, given prohibitive house prices and a lack of private rented property.
• Limited employment opportunities and low wages.
• Lack of public transport.
• Lack of social facilities such as sports, leisure, entertainment.

The surveys in the Llangammarch area uncovered less evidence of perceived deprivation than was found in Corris, and the problems which were being experienced focused on indigenous population groups. The generally low income levels and the limited local employment opportunities affected younger people, and problems relating to limited and inconvenient public transport services were experienced particularly by the elderly.

Source: Cloke and Davies (1992).

---

genuine efforts to integrate themselves by learning the Welsh language, sending their children to the local Welsh-speaking primary school, and so on, there was a conviction amongst Welsh-speaking households that a major part of their 'problem' rested in this cultural sphere.

Equivalent evidence from the Llangammarch Wells study area was subtly different. There was again a greater incidence of low income and opportunity deprivation amongst those households – both elderly and young families – which were indigenous to the area, and incomer groups tended to be relatively affluent and highly mobile. This area, however, does not have the cultural tradition of Welsh speaking that Corris does, and so the interconnection between deprivation and culture was different. Deprivation here was again associated with low income, lack of job choice and lack of accessibility amongst particular groups, and socio-cultural deprivation consisted of the problems experienced in having to travel long distances to cinemas, theatres, recreational and similar facilities.

From this study, Cloke and Davies discerned three main areas in which deprivation and poverty might be thought of as having a specific cultural dimension in rural Wales. First, there is a sense in which cultural groups display particular signs of hardship in rural areas. In this case, 'Welshness' is synonymous with being indigenous to the area, and both young families and elderly households who were indigenous tended to be more marginalized in terms of income, access to housing and mobility than their in-migrant counterparts. Secondly, deprivation includes a sense of denial of reasonable opportunities to pursue various organized aspects of culture. Such aspects are wide-ranging, from the obvious matters of language, poetry, art, literature, drama and music, to the not so obvious cultural arenas such as being able to live comfortably within a heritage, a tradition or even a particular cultural habitat. Thirdly, deprivation involves the experience of feeling culturally marginalized, or threatened, as the nature of a village can change due to the in-migration of particular nationality, class and age groups in an iterative process over time, and can lead to cultural conflict which is perceived to be very much 'part of the problem'. As Cloke and Davies (1992) suggest,

> Conflict can in some places lead to a complete hijack of the existing cultural arena, with different language, organisations and meetings and different interests, idylls and attachments to place dominating what was there previously and becoming common cultural currency. Alternatively, conflict can involve more subtle changes whereby new social groups seek to involve themselves in existing culture, but in doing so change it – in the case of parts of rural Wales such change is reflected in the creeping Anglicisation of previously Welsh-speaking areas. Either way, the cultural arena is transformed, and cultural marginalisation occurs in relative forms for existing groups. (p.357)

As we turn now to the major findings of the Rural Lifestyles surveys on the issues of deprivation and poverty, it will be important to recognize that the specific cultural contexts in rural Wales in which the surveys were undertaken will involve cultural dimensions very important to the experience of low income and poverty.

The Rural Lifestyles study

The question of differential income levels lies at the heart of contemporary accounts of the state of rural Wales in the 1990s. It is assumed that low income represents a vital link in the 'cycle of deprivation' discussed above, and households or individuals with low incomes, whether this represents dependency on state benefit or participation in low-paid employment, are assumed to experience a range of difficulties. These difficulties include: the purchase or rental of housing in rural areas; the purchase and upkeep of personal transport in order to gain access to services and facilities in or nearby urban areas; and 'paying the rural price' for shopping, services, infrastructure and public transport. Low income, then, has been used as a key indicator of a wider set of problems for some rural people.

An interesting facet of the debate on these issues is the relative lack of detailed information on rural income levels. The National Earnings Surveys provide something of a dismal context for an appreciation of income levels in Wales (tables 6.1 and 6.2), with the counties containing the four study areas having earnings which are consistently below the mean for Britain – an 'earnings gap' which widened in 1991, and which shows a marked disparity between male and female earnings. It is against this background that the Rural Lifestyles study was used to construct data on individual and household incomes in our study areas.

At the outset of our discussion of these issues, we would wish to stress that:

- Research to discover and analyse income levels is notoriously difficult and subject to several deficiencies in the construction of accurate data.
- Although the incidence of poverty is certainly of great importance, one essential element of problematic rural lifestyles is the juxtaposition of widely varying incomes. It is therefore necessary to review the spectrum of incomes available to people living in the places concerned.

Asking individuals and households to divulge an accurate statement of their income is one of the most sensitive and difficult parts of social research, often prompting reasonably low response rates. By adopting McLaughlin's (1985) methodology we asked a range of

Table 6.1: Average gross weekly earning of adult male full-time workers, 1981 and 1991, expressed as a percentage of the national mean

	1981	1991
Clwyd West	93.7	83.5
Dyfed (excluding Llanelli)	92.3	80.8
Gwynedd	90.7	83.6
Powys	84.9	77.3
Wales	94.4	87.7
Great Britain	100.0	100.0

Source: National Earnings Survey (1981, 1991).

Table 6.2: Average gross weekly earning of adult female full-time workers, 1981 and 1991, expressed as a percentage of the national mean

	1981	1991	1991 female earnings as %age of male earnings
Clwyd West	nd	85.1	67.7
Dyfed (excluding Llanelli)	91.8	87.0	70.4
Gwynedd	nd	85.9	67.2
Powys	nd	nd	nd
Wales	95.7	89.5	66.5
Great Britain	100.0	100.0	100.0

* nd = no data
Source: National Earnings Survey (1981, 1991).

different questions about income at different times during the interviews with respondents. We requested information on gross annual earnings for each adult member of the household, and for corroborative purposes we also asked respondents for a categorized net household income figure. Response rates varied. Our most userfriendly question (categorized net annual household income) achieved 831 responses from 980 households (84.8 per cent), but our more detailed questions on individual incomes were answered by at worst 8.0 per cent (Betws-y-coed) and at best 18.6 per cent (Tanat Valley) of respondents.

Indications of income levels
Table 6.3 presents data on the reported gross annual earnings for the respondent adult(s) in the households surveyed, and offers an overall profile of income for the entire sample (10.8 per cent earned less than £2,000; 25.6 per cent earned less than £5,000; and so on) and

Table 6.3: Gross annual salary, percentages based on first two adults in household

	Betws-y-coed	Devil's Bridge	Tanat Valley	Teifi Valley	Rural Wales
Up to £1999	20.9	7.8	7.1	9.3	10.8
£2000–£4999	18.2	15.5	15.6	10.0	14.8
£5000–£7999	4.5	17.8	14.3	15.7	13.6
£8000–£14999	27.3	29.5	35.7	26.4	30.3
£15000–£19999	10.0	10.9	7.1	11.4	8.9
£20000–£49999	4.5	10.9	3.2	5.0	5.9
£50000–£99999	0.0	0.0	0.0	0.7	0.2
£100000 or more	0.0	0.0	0.0	0.0	0.0
Refused	5.5	6.2	6.5	10.0	7.2
Don't know	9.1	1.6	10.4	11.4	8.3
Number of responses	110.0	129.0	154.0	135.0	528.0

Table 6.4: Percentage gross annual salaries of first and second adult respondents, below £8,000

Betws-y-coed	43.6	Northumberland	53.4
Devil's Bridge	41.1	North Yorkshire	50.5
Tanat Valley	37.0	Devon	46.9
Teifi Valley	36.3	Shropshire	33.0
All areas	39.2		

individual profiles for the different study areas. It is interesting here to highlight the extremes of the income spectrum in each area. Table 6.4 suggests an important range in the number of respondents in each area on reasonably low incomes. The category of less than £8,000 is used here as a convenient threshold in the categorical data obtained from the surveys. The rank order shows the Betws-y-coed area with the highest number of households in this low-income category, closely followed by the Devil's Bridge area (41.1 per cent). It is also interesting to compare these findings with the four study areas from the English Rural Lifestyles study, selected here for comparison. Three of these areas had higher proportions of residents in this low-income category than were found in the Welsh study areas. Nevertheless, the reported earnings in rural Wales at this modest level are surely significant.

In Table 6.5 we turn to the highest income bands (those above £50,000), and our findings strongly suggest a virtual absence of

Table 6.5: Percentage gross annual salaries of first and second adult respondents, above £50,000, compared with household net income at same level.

	Gross individual income over £50000	Net household income over £50000
Teifi Valley	0.7	0.0
Betws-y-coed	0.0	0.0
Devil's Bridge	0.0	0.5
Tanat Valley	0.0	0.0
All	0.2	0.1
North Yorkshire	0.0	1.3
Devon	0.0	0.8
Northumberland	0.8	1.1
Shropshire	2.2	1.3

high incomes in the four study areas. The table compares the four Wales study areas with four in England where similarly low levels of high income occur, but perhaps a more telling comparison is with the more pressured areas of England studied in the English Rural Lifestyles study, where, for example, West Sussex had 14.6 per cent and Essex had 12.9 per cent of respondents with gross individual incomes in this category. While the choice of indicators can be disputed, there can be little argument that some parts of rural Britain have very many more residents earning high incomes than those in rural Wales.

It might be suggested that it is respondents in these higher income brackets who will be most reluctant to divulge their true earnings. Indeed, it could even be that such reluctance is at its highest in areas where there are fewer other households or individuals evidently earning equivalent incomes. It is useful, therefore, to seek corroboration of these indicators of the level of high incomes in particular areas by comparing them with responses to questions of net household incomes at the same level (£50,000 in this case). This is a different statistic, but in general a similar gradation occurs, and the use of this indicator confirms the virtual absence of high income earners amongst our respondents.

In sum, whereas none of the four Welsh study areas can be characterized as 'high-income areas' there is an indication that the range of low incomes – from 43.6 per cent to 36.3 per cent under £8,000 per annum – does illustrate significant variation. What makes the four study areas different from much of rural England is the lack of juxtapositon of high and low incomes. In many areas of England, the experience of rural lifestyles in terms of material hardship and an inability to pay for important lifestyles opportunities such as access, housing, services, and so on is mixed in with considerable affluence. The four study areas in rural Wales, by comparison, appear to be 'low-income areas' where the juxtaposition with obvious wealth is less pronounced. In relative terms, however, it will be important to use qualitative information to ascertain the degree to which seemingly 'affluent' incomers are perceived as demonstrating 'high-income' lifestyles, and thereby as acting to marginalize existing low-income residents.

Indications of low income and poverty

The literature on poverty in Britain is littered with different definitions of what poverty is and at what income level it is encountered (see, for example, Mack and Lansley, 1985; Oppenheim, 1990; and Walker and Walker, 1987). Our initial analysis of this question of low income and poverty has focused on three standard indicators, which have been widely used in other studies to reflect the 'problem' of poverty. Inevitably, each indicator yields a different picture of the numbers of households experiencing poverty in each area, and of the relative levels of poverty in different study areas. The 'less than 80 per cent of mean and median income' indicators are derived from Bradley et al. (1986) and serve as indices of relative 'poverty', and the 'less than 140 per cent' used by McLaughlin was originally derived from Townsend's (1975, 1979) work on measures of poverty in relation to state benefits.

Most recent work considering low incomes and poverty in rural areas has relied on the 'shorthand' of 25 per cent of households in or on the margins of poverty as popularized by McLaughlin's study. In our Rural Lifestyles analysis, we have maintained the use of the 'up to and including 139 per cent of state benefit' (now income support rather than supplementary benefit as in 1981) indicator. This level of benefit is generally accepted as an indicator of problematic low income and/or poverty by specialist agencies, and is still in use as a critical indicator of poverty (see Townsend, 1993). Townsend (1975, 1979) offers the reasoning for this 140 per cent cut-off level, and makes this an explicit indicator of the margins of poverty in the latter work. State benefit level, or an income equal to it, cannot, Townsend argues, be accepted as a rigid cut-off level for poverty, because of the availability of special needs and necessity payments in addition to basic rate state benefit. These extra payments represent 'practical modificators' not built into any state benefit level (Townsend, 1975, 317). The 140 per cent level derives from Townsend's (1979) subsequent suggestion that

Evidence ... shows that the income for the preceding twelve months of those depending continuously on supplementary benefit, and the income for the preceding week of those receiving supplementary benefit in that week, was often higher than the basic rates plus housing costs. For nearly two thirds of those receiving supplementary benefit it was, in fact, more than 10 per cent higher, and for over a quarter, more than 20 per cent higher, including a minority with an income of 40 per cent higher ... Above [the level of 40 per cent higher than supplementary benefits plus housing costs] only relatively few families in fact prove to be getting help from the [Supplementary Benefits] commission, but the majority of families receiving help have total incomes ranging up to that level. It is also a convenient cutting off point, since it has been used in previous research. (Townsend, 1979, 245)

On these grounds, the validity of the 140 per cent level would appear to have a sound practical and theoretical basis with regard to low-income households. Table 6.6 presents the proportions of households characterized as in or on the margins of poverty according to these three indicators. The first calculates how many households have incomes which are less than 79 per cent of mean household income for that study area. By this indicator, the degree of 'poverty' ranges from 65.2 per cent in the Tanat Valley to 45.1 per cent in Devil's Bridge. Of the Welsh study areas, only Devil's Bridge has lower levels than the four comparable English areas, which range from 61.9 per cent in North Yorkshire to 50.0 per cent in Devon. These findings suggest that according to this indicator, higher levels of households in or on the margins of poverty exist in rural Wales than in the study areas in rural England. According to these definitions, then, there is no question of the problem of low household incomes having disappeared from rural areas such as these during the 1980s.

The second indicator calculates poverty relative to the median income in each study area – a measure which seeks to overcome the

Table 6.6: Percentage of households in or on the margins of poverty definitions: study areas ranked for each of three indicators

Mean*		Median**		Income Support***	
Tanat Valley	65.2	Teifi Valley	36.1	Betws-y-coed	30.0
Betws-y-coed	56.0	Tanat Valley	34.8	Tanat Valley	29.7
Teifi Valley	63.8	Devil's Bridge	33.3	Teifi Valley	26.4
Devil's Bridge	45.1	Betws-y-coed	25.0	Devil's Bridge	25.1
North Yorkshire	61.9	Devon	47.1	Devon	34.4
Northumberland	61.1	North Yorkshire	40.5	Northumberland	26.4
Shropshire	51.4	Northumberland	37.5	North Yorkshire	22.0
Devon	50.0	Shropshire	35.1	Shropshire	21.6

*   In or on the margins of poverty <80% mean.
**   In or on the margins of poverty <80% median.
*** In or on the margins of poverty <140% income support entitlement.

disadvantages of the mean as a measure of central tendency. The proportions of households with less than 80 per cent of the median income for their area are commensurably lower than for the 'mean' index, ranging from 36.1 per cent in the Teifi Valley area to 25.0 per cent in Betws-y-coed. When compared with the four English study areas, these calculations of those in or on the margins of poverty suggest a lower incidence of disadvantage in the Welsh areas – a finding which contradicts the results offered by the 'mean' indicator. Detailed analysis of the actual distributions of income figures in each area would have to be undertaken to explain this statistical anomaly. Despite these differences, the proportions of households thus defined as in or on the margins of poverty remained significantly high, suggesting that between one-quarter and over one-third of households in the Welsh study areas might normatively be associated with poverty according to this indicator.

To some extent, definitions of poverty based purely on income levels can be distorted by other factors such as different housing costs, the presence of large numbers of pensioner households, distinctively high levels of income from savings, and so on. Perhaps, then, a more vigorous indicator of the normative position of a household in or on the margins of poverty is to use Townsend's indicator to assess household income against eligibility for state benefit (in this case income support levels). Table 6.6 shows the proportions of households whose income is less than 140 per cent of income support entitlement, and this is taken as a standard indication of the poverty margin. Using this indicator reduces the proportions of households in or on the margins of poverty still further, and has the effect of identifying more clearly both those areas where poverty so defined is substantially more evident. Thus the 30.0 per cent of households in the Betws-y-coed area and the 29.7 per cent in the Tanat Valley area in this category suggest the presence of particular circumstances which are worthy of specific investigation as contributions to a wider problem which might be labelled 'deprivation'. Indeed, the 26.4 per cent in the Teifi Valley and the 25.1 per cent in Devil's Bridge are not far behind, and equally suggest a significant level of poverty according to this definition. A comparison of these findings with the four English study areas is again revealing. The three Welsh areas with highest levels of poverty according to this indicator have an equal or greater proportion of households so characterized than any English study areas apart from Devon. There is certainly a greater scale of problem suggested in Betws-y-coed, Tanat Valley and Teifi Valley than in the North Yorkshire and Shropshire study areas, where it might be thought that the same types and scale of problems would occur.

Three notes of caution should immediately be attached to these interpretative comments.

(1) The fact that all four study areas contain over 25 per cent households in or close to poverty itself suggests a severe problem of rural lifestyle in most areas of the country.

(2) There appears to be a mix of rural geographies at work here. Although throughout our study of rural lifestyles in England and Wales the more urbanized study areas tend to have lower proportions of households categorized by this index and the more remote areas tend to have higher proportions, the range of 'poverty' findings here – from 34.4 per cent in Devon to 25.1 per cent in Devil's Bridge and 21.6 per cent in Shropshire indicates that such tendencies are subject to alteration by local circumstances. We need to look beyond recourse merely to all-encompassing structural factors or to broad concepts such as 'remoteness' or 'pressure' in the understanding of these phenomena.

(3) It has been argued that issues of poverty and deprivation are somehow phenomena of a previous time-period, becoming anachronistic in the 'prosperity' of the 1980s. Our findings

Table 6.7: Percentage of households moving into the area over the last five years with incomes under £8,000 or above £20,000 per annum

	under £8000		over £20000
Teifi Valley	33.5	Tanat Valley	6.3
Devil's Bridge	29.0	Teifi Valley	6.9
Betws-y-coed	25.7	Betws-y-coed	8.1
Tanat Valley	25.6	Devil's Bridge	14.2
Northumberland	36.6	Devon	4.6
North Yorkshire	29.2	Northumberland	7.6
Shropshire	26.1	Shropshire	20.3
Devon	24.8	North Yorkshire	25.4

suggest that the issue is not only very significant and important in our 1991 surveys but is also being reproduced by patterns of in-migration to particular places.

Table 6.7 demonstrates the connection between households moving into different study areas during the five years previous to the survey, and income levels. In each of the Welsh study areas, more than 25 per cent of in-migrant households have low incomes (using a measure in this case of household incomes under £8,000). Indeed in Teifi Valley more than one-third of in-migrants are so categorized. These findings match the situations in the four English study areas. Problems associated with low income and poverty are therefore being reproduced in these 'low-income' areas through processes of in-migration. The reverse is true of in-migrants with high household incomes (measured here as above £20,000). Three of the Welsh areas have less than 10 per cent high-income in-migrants; the fourth, Devil's Bridge, has just under 15 per cent. These proportions are significantly less than were found in Shropshire and North Yorkshire, although they tally with the findings in Devon and Northumberland. The study areas in rural Wales, then, may be regarded as amongst those places with the smallest number of affluent in-migrants, and this appears to be an essential characteristic of the reproduction of economic and social relations in these areas.

Indications of the anatomy of poverty
As part of the Rural Lifestyles study, a further analysis was undertaken of those households which were categorized as being in or on

the margins of poverty, using the income support definition (Table 6.6). The idea here is to understand something of an 'anatomy' of impoverished households in each area, so as to investigate whether similar household characteristics occur throughout the study areas or whether particular localities exhibit specific forms of poverty. This analysis deals with low numbers of households (a total of 144, that is 14.7 per cent of our sample) because the low response rates to our questions about income mean that although the percentage of those who did respond to be found in or on the margins of poverty is high, the actual number of households concerned is small in each case. The following summary of findings should be set in this context, but it does suggest some very interesting indications of the geography of rural problems associated with poverty.

The types of households categorized as being in or on the margins of poverty were dominated in three out of the four study areas by elderly people. Single elderly people are a major group of those in or on the margins of poverty in areas such as Betws-y-coed, and a mixture of single and two-person elderly households, were characteristic of this measure of poverty in Tanat Valley and Teifi Valley. These findings confirm those in the English study which suggest that some elderly people in rural areas are prone to problems of poverty caused by low income, perhaps having to rely on state pensions for their lifestyle. As might be expected given greater longevity amongst women, there was a predominance of women amongst the elderly poor. Rural poverty thus defined is not, however, universally a characteristic of elderly households. The Devil's Bridge study area showed noticeably different households in poverty, specifically younger single-person households, and two-person households with ages ranging from their thirties to their fifties.

The occurrence of poverty amongst these households was mixed between newcomers and those who were well established in the areas concerned. In the Betws-y-coed area, it was established elderly residents who were impoverished. The Teifi Valley area also had long-standing households in poverty, but also some who had lived in the area for less than fifteen years. The households in poverty in the Devil's Bridge area displayed a mixed length of residence, and interestingly, the Tanat Valley households in this category included a significant group of newly arrived retirees. Apart from in Betws-y-coed, at least half of these households had kin nearby, suggesting either that poverty is associated with 'local' families or individuals, or that some elderly people moving in to be near family are being categorized by this analysis.

The housing characteristics associated with households in poverty are also interesting. The incidence of dwellings with four rooms or fewer was high in Betws-y-coed and to a lesser extent Teifi Valley, and proportionally more such households reported housing defects than was found in the survey of lifestyles in rural England. Poverty then is at least in part associated with small, poor-quality housing. Housing-tenure mix varied between areas, with the Betws-y-coed households, for example, all living in fully owned dwellings, but with local authority tenancies accounting for nearly half of the households in Devil's Bridge and Tanat Valley. In the Teifi Valley area, most of the households concerned were renting from the local authority.

The numbers of households identified in this analysis where at least one member was in employment was relatively small, especially given the dominance of the elderly poor as mentioned above. However, an analysis of the job types represented indicates a range of different employment sectors. This gives an indication that at least some of those households experiencing problems associated with poverty in rural areas are in low-paid employment, especially in the service sector, and perhaps can be counted amongst the 'working poor' of rural Wales.

Much has been made in previous studies of the relationship between poverty and non-mobility (see chapter 5). The households defined as in or on the margins of poverty in this analysis vary in their access to a car at all times. In Betws-y-coed and the Teifi Valley, households in or near poverty are significantly associated with lack of access to a car. These areas are notably those which are in relative terms the most accessible of the four study areas. In Devil's Bridge and the Tanat Valley, which are far less accessible, there are much lower rates of lack of access to a car. Perhaps here the option to pursue a low-income rural lifestyle without a car is commensurately harder, and households either became reluctant car owners or face the prospect of moving to a more accessible place. The relationship between access and poverty is at least partly linked with the incidence of the 'elderly poor' and the 'working poor', but it is also subject to localized factors such as the varying availability of local services and public transport.

Table 6.8: Percentages of respondents who thought that disadvantage or deprivation did occur in rural areas

Betws-y-coed	40.8	Northumberland	36.3
Devil's Bridge	61.5	North Yorkshire	46.2
Tanat Valley	33.3	Devon	43.9
Teifi Valley	41.2	Shropshire	39.8
All	43.7		

This brief analysis of the anatomy of poverty as found in our surveys indicates that there are significant local differences in the relationship between poverty and social groups, housing characteristics, economic activity and mobility. Although the 'problem' of low income is common to all by definition, there is little evidence of the classic deprivation of income, household and opportunity as discussed earlier in this chapter. Rather, individuals and households on low incomes seem likely to experience their lifestyle differently according to local housing, service, job and access markets. Their experience of rural lifestyles will also be affected by less tangible social and cultural ideas of conflict, change and power, and it is to these matters that we turn next.

Indications of the experience of income and status issues

In outlining our approach to presenting the findings of this study (chapter 1) we stressed the need to combine information about rural lifestyles from the perspective of both the outside looking in, and the inside looking out. Despite the indication of the existence of low income and poverty discussed above, it is important to supplement our understanding of these issues with an interpretation of what our respondents said about the influence of low and high income on rural lifestyles. When asked whether disadvantage or deprivation occurred in rural areas, an average of 43.7 per cent answered in the affirmative, ranging between study areas from 61.5 per cent in Devil's Bridge to 33.3 per cent in the Tanat Valley (see table 6.8). These findings are in line with the degree of deprivation perceived by respondents in the four English counties, except for the very high level found in the Devil's Bridge area, where particular local characteristics appear to be important. There is no apparent association between levels of low income and perceived deprivation in the study areas.

Those respondents who did perceive a problem of rural disadvantage or deprivation pointed to conventional issues relating to low income and lack of opportunities as well as to the problems experienced by different groups of people:

> The only deprivation is for the low-paid who can't find appropriate housing. (1025, Betws-y-coed)

> Low incomes, transport not too great, got to have your own car if you want to have work in other areas. (1146, Betws-y-coed)

> People are deprived because of lack of services. (2215, Devil's Bridge)

> People just lose out because of lack of transport. (2204, Devil's Bridge)

> Lot of old people in very poor conditions. (4138, Teifi Valley)

> Some young people suffer disadvantage being cut off in such a rural village. (3027, Tanat Valley)

> In this area there is certainly deprivation amongst blue-collar workers ... deprivation in terms of leisure facilities and money to enjoy leisure. (2092, Devil's Bridge)

Indeed from the qualitative text in the survey it is possible to discern particular problems experienced by residents of particular study areas – notably housing problems in the Teifi Valley and problems with medical services in the Tanat Valley.

On the other hand, qualitative information from the surveys also offers several explanations as to why perception levels of rural disadvantage and deprivation are not higher. The stigma associated with these problems was rarely mentioned, but the idea that problems of deprivation are hidden from rural residents did come through very clearly:

> I don't think there is really deprivation in rural areas nowadays. (1062, Betws-y-coed)

> There are also homeless people here but they are invisible. (2058, Devil's Bridge)

> Deprivation probably does exist but we don't see that much. (2220, Devil's Bridge)

Don't think there is deprivation – villagers look after one another. (3028, Tanat Valley)

No sign of it [poverty] around here; people may be, but hide it. (4146, Teifi Valley)

Some views on this issue claimed that deprivation was a non-issue simply because the 'undeserving poor' were failing to help themselves:

People should move to towns to find employment. (1236, Betws-y-coed)

People should get off their arses and get to work. (1026, Betws-y-coed)

Deprived people move here and get council houses; they can't better this situation. (1244, Betws-y-coed)

Those who claim to be deprived would have a lot better life if they spent less time in the pub and quit smoking. (3119, Tanat Valley)

I think it's self-created poverty. (4146, Teifi Valley)

In other responses, it becomes clear that deprivation is not thought to exist because country life is thought to be a different material and symbolic experience from town life.

Yes, there's deprivation of the things which a town can offer, but people have chosen to live here exactly for that reason. (3187, Tanat Valley)

We don't want anything really. I suppose if you haven't got a car the buses should be better, but you wouldn't live here without a car would you? (2059, Devil's Bridge)

Interestingly, some respondents noted a difference in the symbolic qualities of English and Welsh rural life:

Well that's a very interesting question. What do you mean by rural? As an Englishman I tend to think to cosy little villages but yes, yes there are no centres of population or industry. (2052, Devil's Bridge)

Many other respondents regarded rural dwellers as having lower expectations than their urban counterparts, thus rendering the lack of particular opportunities less than problematic in some cases:

> Live a simpler life, don't expect the things, e.g. theatre; don't worry about clothes, figures, etc. (4136, Teifi Valley)

> Compared to Liverpool, you can hide away here and shut yourself off. (4132, Teifi Valley)

The other side of the coin to these lower expectations is that rural areas provide some residents with a form of psychic income which compensates in some cases for the lack of other opportunities and facilities:

> Where people are deprived of services they make up in other areas (beauty, quiet) which towns are deprived of. (3056, Tanat Valley)

> Because of clean surroundings people are less likely to suffer chest complaints, etc. (1242, Betws-y-coed)

> Living here your mind is pure; it follows that your body must be. (3026, Tanat Valley)

> More relaxed, better for your nerves, people not at each other's throats. (3243, Tanat Valley)

> I enjoy the Welshness – countryside and agricultural community – farmers for friends. (3200, Tanat Valley)

> No high-rise flats, no motorways, no noise, no industry. (2210, Devil's Bridge)

> Don't get mugged, no large factories, wind comes straight off the sea. (4007, Teifi Valley)

Such experiences contrast with the 'psychic taxation' (i.e. the opposite of psychic income) relating to negative lifestyle experiences in the rural areas:

> Different problems in the country – more exposed to the natural elements. High cases of cancer in the village due to lead from mountains in atmosphere and water. (3188, Tanat Valley)

There's a lot of people who think they have the right to judge what you do and to discuss it endlessly. People think of kindly neighbours leaving eggs at the back door, but here they'd probably be off. (2196, Devil's Bridge)

I sometimes feel as if I'm living with a circus. It would be nice to have something of our own for a change rather than a travelling doctor, a travelling vet and so on. (3056, Tanat Valley)

[Need] improved water supply, improved telephone lines, improvement in the pollution of rivers in the area ... improvement in police services ... (2186, Devil's Bridge)

Out in the sticks with no hospital immediately on hand there should be more medical services if anything. (3187, Tanat Valley)

One major finding of our qualitative studies on these issues was that the experience of having or lacking income is very much wrapped up in respondents' minds with their interpretations of the status of powerful groups in their village or area. This is not to suggest that money equals power for all rural people. Rather, our suggestion is that the experience of low household income, or indeed of a more affluent lifestyle, occurs in a context of the cultural, political and economical choices afforded to particular groups in that place. A few respondents denied that any particular social group was dominant in their area:

Class is more pronounced in affluent areas, not much in rural areas. (4192, Teifi Valley)

Country people have learnt how to live together. They are more responsible to and for each other – going to a church or chapel helps this. (3203, Tanat Valley)

Many others, however, readily identified the importance of status in assessing the powers and powerlessness of different groups in village affairs:

Way of life and attitudes differ with income, wealth and power. (4200, Teifi Valley)

Many, for example, suggested that the importance of status and class in Welsh rural areas has to be seen in a different light from what applies in England:

I think that class in Welsh society is different from that in England society. In Wales the highest class is the educated, in England it's to do with wealth and power. (1222, Betws-y-coed)

[It is] only in England that you get class. Here, in the pub the professor drinks with the labourer. We've had class from the southern English and we see class distinction as an English way of life and attitude. (4136, Teifi Valley)

Nevertheless, there were clear indications from the survey that both wealth and landedness were important social forces in at least some of the study areas:

First order of division is those who have and those who haven't. Then there are the sub-orders – those that have inherited wealth, those who have made it themselves, those that aspire to be great and arse-lick everyone else, those who had no money but work hard and don't get anywhere, those who have had money but lost it, and those that have never had it and are never going to have it. (2058, Devil's Bridge)

There are people with money in the area but they are not as wealthy as elsewhere, not so stuck up. People with money and who own property have power. (2075, Devil's Bridge)

Class distinction is more acute in Wales although they don't admit it – between farmers and workers. The situation is overlain with chapel – adds a level of confusion to it. (2097, Devil's Bridge)

Landowners are still quite respected in the village. Gentry are looked up to. (3024, Tanat Valley)

Wealthy landowners such as our MP who is a sheep farmer. Councillors often own land too. (2074, Devil's Bridge)

In rural areas the upper class may not be extremely rich but they are respected and looked up to because they are that breed known as landowners. (3119, Tanat Valley)

Can't tell whether people have money or not; some all look the same ... Hierarchies in terms of power exist but are not immediately obvious to outsiders. (2079, Devil's Bridge)

The relevance of experiencing a rural lifestyle on a certain income amongst these various contexts of status and dominant social groups lies in the interconnection between economic power and social and cultural power in rural life. Rural people reflect on their own income positions in terms of the power structures around them, as well as in the more specific terms of what opportunities or facilities can be obtained or denied because of spending power. In English rural areas, our surveys found that perceived choice and opportunity were dominated by existing wealthy classes and, very importantly, in-migrant groups. In this study of rural Wales, the role of English in-migrants was such that the dominant focus of social and cultural relations of power was the effect of 'the English' in rural communities. Despite the fact that political power is usually retained by local people,

> The hub of the community has amazingly managed to remain despite outsiders. (3187, Tanat Valley)

> Welsh have strong hold on council. (4138, Teifi Valley)

The most significant factor in the study areas was what 'the English' were doing to rural life and lifestyle. Concerns ranged from housing issues to the way in which in-migrants were usurping language, culture and community:

> Some English come here and act like colonials, talk about us as peasants. (4138, Teifi Valley)

> English immigrants have forced the Welshness – the general character of Llangynog – to change. (3054, Tanat Valley)

> English people moving in are bound to have an effect – more strangers so less of a friendly spirit. (2205, Devil's Bridge)

> English people have moved in and are trying to dominate the bloody country. It is wrong. (3222, Tanat Valley)

> Many are low-paid or unemployed or elderly and can't compete with affluent immigrants. It's up to the council and politicians to stop the flooding of rural areas with get-rich-quick English businessmen. (1112, Betws-y-coed)

> The English are affecting the prices. Selling houses in London and such and buying here. (4056, Teifi Valley)

English have moved into the area. Few houses in the village are now anything more than holiday homes. (3054, Tanat Valley)

Escalated local prices of housing – beyond the means of local people. The locality is losing its character. Local children are losing their first language. (4198, Teifi Valley)

Conclusions

At the beginning of this chapter, we suggested that to provide an account of the experience of low income and poverty in rural Wales was by no means a straightforward task. Aside from the methodological difficulties in presenting convincing measurements and categorizations of poverty, the idea that deprivation or poverty represents a major problem in the contemporary countryside is challenged by a range of cultural assumptions about the nature and significance of rural lifestyles. For example, especially since the population 'turnaround' of the 1970s and 1980s, and the consequent fading of the problematic spectre of depopulation, there has been a common assumption that migration into rural Wales has brought with it a generalized atmosphere of prosperity. Such an assumption is reinforced by the spread of the more English Thatcherite transformation of public discourses about rurality, which increasingly paint rural areas as unproblematic idylls. It is equally reinforced by more traditional but equally persuasive ideas which suggest that privation of resources and opportunities in rural areas is somehow compensated by the 'psychic income' derived from the beauty of the surrounding landscape and nature. Moreover, in rural Wales the suggestion remains that traditional rural lifestyles – and this may tacitly include poverty and deprivation – represent something of a bastion against the threat of Englishness to the living indigenous culture, especially to language and to a form of democratic classlessness.

The Rural Lifestyles study does add considerable weight to the suggestion of a continuing significance of low income in many rural areas. Statistics drawn from the Townsend indicator, which point to 30 per cent of households in the Betws-y-coed study area, 29.7 per cent in the Tanat Valley, 26.4 per cent in the Teifi Valley and 25.1 per cent in the Devil's Bridge study areas as being in, or on the margins of, poverty, appear to us to be of considerable importance.

In these areas there is a strong case for suggesting that a significant minority of households in the countryside have income levels which may create difficulties for them in the purchase of housing, mobility, leisure activities and a host of other opportunities.

Although any threshold on such an indicator of poverty is likely to be arguable politically, it also seems significant to us that each study area contained 25 per cent or more households classified by this indicator as being in or on the margins of poverty. Such levels were, for example, at least *twice* as high as unemployment levels, which are themselves often used as a 'litmus test' of an area's prosperity, and which often elicit specific policy responses. Our study shows that there is, at an aggregate level, a very important problem of low income and poverty in rural areas of Wales.

Not only was there a significant presence of low-income households in the rural Wales study areas, but the presence of 'have-nots' in these places was not in any way receding. Poverty and low income are not yesterday's problems in rural Wales. Each of the study areas had recently received a significant proportion of lower-income in-migrants, and it may, therefore, also be suggested that the problems associated with low income and poverty were being reproduced more generally across rural Wales. Nevertheless, our respondents were, on the whole, reluctant to admit the existence of poverty and deprivation in their areas. Although an average of 43.7 per cent did perceive that disadvantage and deprivation existed in their areas, the qualitative comments from our survey suggested that the notion of deprivation was stigmatic for some of our respondents, and often 'out of sight, out of mind' for others. It would seem that the perceived benefits of living in the countryside were felt to offer some compensation for those people who might otherwise find a low-income lifestyle a severe problem. Equally, however, the supposed compensations of the rural idyll were not shared by all, and living in a rural environment can itself be a problem for some rural residents regardless of income.

Finally, it is clear from these surveys that 'deprivation' and 'disadvantage' entail both material and socio-cultural characteristics. The experience of lack of income can be compounded when new dominant social groups exert their power and economic status so as to deny others the continuing opportunity to belong – socially, culturally and even sometimes politically – to their desired rural lifestyles in their desired rural place. The denial of belonging in rural Wales is clearly discernible in the knowing or unknowing imposition by in-migrants of different cultural ideas of what rural life should be like on existing rural residents. Some in-migrants appear to be attempting, conscientiously, to acquire the cultural competences which would both help them to belong and prevent the non-belonging of local Welsh people. This process means more than just learning a language (although many of our respondents applauded those in-migrants who were doing so); it means learning a new set of cultural constructs about rurality, idyll and rural community life in Wales. For both indigenous Welsh people and in-migrant English people, the cultural conflicts, contests and incompetences occurring in rural Wales present a very significant source of symbolic disadvantage and marginalization which interconnects in a complex manner with more material issues of income and wealth. These issues are pursued further in chapter 7.

References

Archbishops' Commission on Rural Areas (1990) *Faith in the Countryside*, Churchman, Worthing.

Bowen, E. G. (1957) *Wales: A Physical, Historical and Regional Geography*, Methuen, London.

Bradley, T., Lowe, P. and Wright, S. (1986) 'Introduction: rural deprivation and welfare', in P. Lowe, T. Bradley, and S. Wright (eds.), *Deprivation and Welfare in Rural Areas*, Geobooks, Norwich.

Cloke, P. (1993) 'On "problems and solutions": the reproduction of problems for rural communities in Britain during the 1980's', *Journal of Rural Studies*, 9, 113–21.

Cloke, P. (1995) 'Rural poverty and the welfare state: a discursive transformation in Britain and the USA', *Environment and Planning A*, 27, 1001–16.

Cloke, P. (1996) 'Rural lifestyles: material opportunity, cultural experience, and how theory can undermine policy?', *Economic Geography*, 72, 433–49.

Cloke, P. and Davies, L. (1992) 'Deprivation and lifestyles in rural Wales', I: 'Towards a cultural dimension', *Journal of Rural Studies* 8, 349–58.

Cloke, P., Goodwin, M., Milbourne, P. and Thomas, C. (1995) 'Deprivation, poverty and marginalisation in rural lifestyles in England and Wales', *Journal of Rural Studies*, 11, 351–65.

Cloke, P. and Milbourne, P. (1992) 'Deprivation and lifestyles in rural

Wales', II: 'Rurality and the cultural dimension', *Journal of Rural Studies*, 8, 360–74.

Cloke, P., Milbourne, P. and Thomas, C. (1995) 'Poverty in the country-side: out of sight and out of mind', in C. Philo (ed.), *Off the Map: The Social Geography of Poverty*, Child Poverty Action Group, London.

Fabes, R., Worsley, L. and Howard, M. (1983) *The Myth of the Rural Idyll*, Child Poverty Action Group, Leicester.

Fleure, H. (1941) Foreword, in E. Bowen, *Wales: A Study in Geography and History*, University of Wales Press Board, Cardiff.

Matless, D. (1994) 'Doing the English village, 1945–1990: an essay in imaginative geography', in P. Cloke, M. Doel, D. Matless, M. Phillips, and N. Thrift (eds.), *Writing the Rural: Five Cultural Geographies*, Paul Chapman, London.

McLaughlin, B. (1985) *Deprivation in Rural Areas*, research report to the Department of the Environment.

McLaughlin, B. (1986) 'The rhetoric and reality of rural deprivation', *Journal of Rural Studies*, 2, 291–307.

Milbourne, P. (1996) 'Hidden from view: poverty and marginalisation in rural Britain', in P. Milbourne (ed.), *Revealing Rural 'Others'*, Cassell, London.

Mingay, G. (ed.) (1989a) *The Rural Idyll*, Routledge, London.

Mingay, G. (ed.) (1989b) *The Unquiet Countryside*, Routledge, London.

Mingay, G. (ed.) (1989c) *The Vanishing Countryman*, Routledge, London.

Mingione, E. (1993) 'The new urban poverty and the underclass: introduction', *International Journal of Urban and Regional Research*, 17, 324–6.

Roberts, L. (1992) 'A rough guide to rurality', *Association of Community Workers, Newcastle-upon-Tyne, Talking Point*, 137, 1–6.

Scott, D., Shenton, N. and Healey, B. (1991) *Hidden Deprivation in the Countryside*, Report to the Peak Park Trust.

Shaw, M. (ed.) (1979) *Rural Deprivation and Planning*, Geobooks, Norwich.

Thomas, D. (ed.) (1977) *Wales: A New Study*, David and Charles, Newton Abbot.

Thomas, D. E. (1988) 'Ridding Wales of a siege mentality', *Western Mail*, 9 July.

Townsend, P. (1975) *Sociology and Social Policy*, Penguin, Harmondsworth.

Townsend, P. (1979) *Poverty in the United Kingdom*, Allen Lane, London.

Townsend, P. (1993) *The International Analysis of Poverty*, Harvester Wheatsheaf, London.

Walker, A. (ed.) (1978) *Rural Poverty*, Child Poverty Action Group, London.

Wenger, C. (1980) *Mid-Wales: Deprivation or Development*, University of Wales Press, Cardiff.

Wyn Jones, I. (1991) 'Policies for the Welsh countryside: Plaid Cymru', *Rural Wales* (Summer).

7 • Community and Environment in Welsh Rural Lifestyles

Introduction

> Since I came to live in Cwmrheidol seven years ago countless people
> have said to me, 'You are lucky to live in such a beautiful place'. If they
> are visitors, they usually add, 'But don't you feel cut off – it's so
> remote?' If they are incomers like myself they want to know how I have
> settled down in a local community which is increasingly a mix of Welsh
> speaking local people and English speaking incomers. If they are locals
> they may express gladness that another empty old house has once again a
> light in the window and smoke rising from the chimney. Or they may see
> me as a statistic in the flow of incomers ... whose arrival changes the
> character of entire villages and hastens the demise of a fragile Welsh
> rural culture. (Jones, 1993, 9)

In this chapter, we want to examine a little more closely some of
the issues raised so eloquently by Noragh Jones. In particular, we
are seeking to trace how experiences of 'well-being' and 'belonging' in Welsh rural lifestyles are attributable to affinities with
community and environment leading to experiences of unwell-being
and non-belonging. Our interest in these issues follows on from
previous concerns expressed in this book, especially the experiences
of social and cultural change discussed in chapter 2, and the
recognition in chapter 6 that poverty and marginalization reflect not
only the structuring of income, resources and opportunities, but
also more experiential factors relating to 'not fitting in' with local
cultural constructions of rurality and community.

Before introducing the findings from the Rural Lifestyles study,
we want to explore some of the rich heritage of 'community' and
(to a lesser extent) 'nature' research in rural Wales. In separating
these two aspects of potential rural well-being, we reaffirm that
they are in fact closely interconnected. In Rapport's (1993) account
of the diversity and ambiguity of socio-cultural interaction in
'Wanet', a village in Cumbria, he stresses the close links between
everyday community life and the everyday landscapes of the dale:

As the local proverbial wisdom has it: 'Kick one person from Wanet and next day seven people will be limping'. In this narrow valley, exchange of information, albeit along particular routes, is rapid and regular, and feelings of belonging prevalent. For here is a collection of people linked together closely, possessing many of the same names for pertinent landmarks in their cognitive maps of everyday landscapes. And yet they are not linked by any singular or imperative status. Rather, the dale of Wanet can be seen as an assemblage of individual lives which influence, overlap and abut against one another in a number of ways. (p.43)

It is this close yet diverse assemblage of nature–society relations which forms an important arena for the understanding of belonging and well-being (or their opposites) in rural areas.

Community and belonging

Butler-Flora et al. (1992) suggest that rural community has at its heart a shared sense of place, and that initially this sense of place had a social as well as a geographical meaning. Thus traditional accounts of rural communities described the coming together of location, social system and common identity, in which localized sets of social institutions ensured that people's needs could be met in an environment which fostered a shared sense of identity. However, whereas the rural landscape has stayed *relatively* stable over the past century, the growth of communication, transportation and information technology has meant that the geographical localization of these interactions has been fragmented by numerous centrifugal forces, as a result of which rural people travel far outside their locale for work, services and facilities as well as for leisure and other social interaction. Nevertheless, as Butler-Flora et al. stress,

Despite these changes, a sense of place still figures prominently in a definition of country. Many rural residents maintain an emotional and symbolic attachment to the community in which they live. (p.15)

The continuing importance of rural community, regardless of the impact of modernizing changes, has to do with the symbolic construction and reconstruction of community over successive generations and through dynamic circumstances. The work of Anthony Cohen (1982, 1985, 1987) is important here. Cohen has argued that rural communities are best understood in terms of 'communities of meaning' rather than material social interaction. Community is thus seen to play a symbolic role in constructing and sustaining a sense of belonging which relies on the perceived vitality of community culture. Belonging is enhanced by the drawing of boundaries which discriminate between the community and other places and groups, and thus it is the imagined community which differentiates between those local identities which are shared and those which are different (see also Roberts, 1992). As Crow and Allen (1994) conclude:

> communities are defined not only by relations between members, among whom there is similarity, but also by the relations between these 'insiders' and 'outsiders' who are distinguished by their difference and consequent exclusion. (p.7)

Rural Wales benefits from having been the subject of a rich tapestry of community studies since 1940. These include the seminal contributions of

- Rees (1950) on Llanfihangel-yng-Ngwynfa (Montgomeryshire)
- Frankenberg (1957) on Llansanffraid Glynceiriog (Denbighshire)
- Jenkins (1960) on Aber-porth (Cardiganshire)
- Jones (1960) on Tregaron (Cardiganshire)
- Hughes (1960) on Aberdaron (Caernarfonshire)
- Owen (1960) on Glan-llyn (Merioneth)
- Emmett (1964) on Llanfrothen (Merioneth)
- Madgwick et al. (1973) on Cardiganshire

and have more recently been added to by Day and Murdoch (1993) in Montgomeryshire and Jones (1993) in Cwmrheidol (Ceredigion). Although each of these studies was quite distinctive in character, they may in part be summarized as emphasizing that 'true' rurality is always associated with geographical peripherality – where identity, language and way of life foster both simple and symbolic community – and that modernization is always at work, turning simple society into more complex society (see Wright, 1992). We can thus suggest that community in these rural areas is at least in part constructed through a combination of negative comparisons with the rural past, and positive comparisons with the urban modernizing present. Rees (1950) explains this point in terms of the people of Llanfihangel:

Their invariable answer to the question whether any of the traditional features survive today is: 'No, nothing like what it used to be'. And they will explain that in these days people are too preoccupied with their own affairs to be neighbourly, too busy to visit and entertain, in too much of a hurry to tarry and talk. It is *myna* (going, movement) that appeals to the young and the rest are too busy 'scratching' for money to live the leisurely life of the old days. Again they will point to the emptiness of the chapels and churches, and the older ones will insist that the standards of concerts, eisteddfodau and Sunday Schools are much lower and the preparation for them much more perfunctory than in former times. And the evidence they adduce proves that they are not just romanticising their own youth. *Judged by urban standards the culture retains many of its old characteristics; judged by its own past it is in full decline.* (p.168, our emphasis).

The symbolic construction of belonging (or not) to and in these communities is equally important in these studies of rural Wales. Sometimes, belonging is associated baldly with length of residence. Rees, for example, noted that an individual would be counted as a stranger unless his or her family had resided in that community for at least two generations. This suggestion is echoed in the more recent study by Day and Murdoch (1993) who noted without surprise that in-migrants of fifteen years' standing were still not perceived as belonging to the local community. Given that many studies contextualize the changing rural community in terms of very long-term accretions (for example, Jones, 1950, on Tregaron talks about 'the Victorian accretions of the last century' as being still 'neither finally accepted or rejected' – p.114), these time-scales of belonging are unsurprising.

Nevertheless, length of residence is only part of the symbolic differentiation between inclusion and exclusion in Welsh rural communities. Perhaps the overriding moment of differentiation concerns 'Welshness'. Madgwick et al. (1973), for example, conclude that

> there is a 'Welsh culture' in Cardiganshire, and that 'this specifically Welsh cultural activity is reinforced by strong subjective identification with Welshness. (p.85)

Here, then, we have reference to the perhaps more obvious practices and language of Welsh cultural activity, but also to a series of assumed national characteristics of rural Welsh people which (as suggested by Cohen) are honed in relation to alternative characteristics of Englishness. Figure 7.1 summarizes some of these characteristics.

Figure 7.1: Madgwick et al.'s findings on Welshness and Englishness in rural Cardiganshire

Welsh community living
'The Welsh are more in-bred.'
'The Welsh are more clannish.'
'Welsh people cling together more than the English.'
'The Welsh have a different attitude to living. They live closer together.'
'More of a communal existence really. Everyone will talk to you. You can run in and out of each other's houses.'
'The Welshmen are more busy-bodies.'
'The Welsh are more homely, closer to you.'
'It's really all part of the same family and total influence. We tend to take a communal interest in everyone else's fortune, good or bad, e.g. funerals – the whole village attends, and ministers of all denominations in the locality take part.'

Friendliness of the Welsh
'Welsh are more friendly.'
'Welshmen are friendlier, easier to get on with, and they don't stand aloof. English people are all right once you get to know them.'
'Welsh are very friendly, accept you if you make the first move, and then you're one of them.'
'Welsh are more homely.'

Welsh community participation
'Welsh keener on local affairs than the English.'
'Welsh social life different – more participation, make more of their own entertainment.'

The English
'English are more independent, aloof.'
'English homes not so open as Welsh homes.'
'In London you would not know your next-door neighbour.'
'The English are more stand-offish, and they don't bother if anyone needs help. When I stayed in Luton, a woman was screaming blue murder in a home across the street and nobody took any notice – she could have been killed.'
'When an Englishman buys a home in Wales, the first thing he does is to put up a notice: "Private. No parking."'

Source: Madgwick et al. (1973), 88–9.

As Madgwick et al. note, their respondents were almost entirely in favour of the outlooks associated with Welshness rather than those of Englishness. Perhaps the exception to this is the suggestion that Welsh rural communities can be claustrophobic – as suggested by terms such as 'clannish' and 'in-bred'.

One of the major messages of community studies in rural Wales, then, is to suggest that symbolic characteristics of community, which differentiate between those who belong and those who do not, tend to interconnect in two ways relating to being Welsh. First, there is a difference relating to a Welsh 'culture', reflecting the popular spoken and musical cultures traditionally formed around the chapel and the Eisteddfod, but continually regenerating in appropriate cultural and political containers which reflect the contemporary nature of the Welsh nation. Secondly, there is a sense of being Welsh, which is defined at least in part by the opposition to 'being English'.

We would further wish to suggest that these two axes of Welshness continue to represent arenas of potential well-being/belonging or unwell-being/unbelonging in contemporary rural Wales. This is not some simple reductionist thesis of inevitable conflict between Welsh and English with the inevitable result that Englishness cannot be equated with any sense of belonging in the context of rural Wales. Clearly, different individuals and house-holds moving into rural Wales will (consciously or unconsciously) have different strategies for coping with the questions of assimilation. Similarly, long-standing indigenous Welsh residents will respond differently to these people and their strategies. However it may well be that the reasons for in-migration are fuelled by assumptions about rural life drawn from English community, rurality and nature which may be more or less incompatible with attributes of Welshness. Both Englishness and Welshness find expression in sense of place, in convictions or dreams about the nature of small-scale living, in desiring a sense of place-identity and in a sharing of common habitat and interests. However, they do so differently in many cases. Noragh Jones (1993) quotes from two differentiated attitudes encountered in her study:

> It's [a] shock to find that even when the Welsh and the English speak the same language, we do not mean the same things. (p.325)

It's a shock to find that though you are not leaving your culture, your culture is leaving you. (p.325)

She notes the traumatic experiences which occur when Welshness meets Englishness and vice versa, and whether the coping strategies of in-migrants involve a joining in, or a form of cultural apartheid. She illustrates how different communities are sharing the same locality, busily stereotyping each other in a 'them and us' manner. Her message of the need to build bridges and construct dialogues about a common shared future serves to give further emphasis to the gulf to be spanned by those bridges and dialogues:

At one extreme that would defuse Meibion Glyndwr's arson attacks on English owned houses and businesses. At another extreme it would de-ghettoise the many incomers who never get to know any Welsh people beyond the formal courtesies of daily greeting. (p.325)

Community, then, is built upon a series of cultural competences which in the context of rural Wales are not easily learned by English in-migrants bringing with them very different competences based on very different models of rural community. We return to this theme later in this chapter.

Environment and belonging

The second aspect potentially contributing to experiences of well-being and belonging in Welsh rural lifestyles is an affinity with the environment in the localities concerned. Here we can trace a broader prompt to the decision of many urban-to-rural migrants in terms of a wish to leave behind the concrete jungle of the city and find a lifestyle which incorporates broader expanses of landscape, a healthier environment and a closeness to nature. For some, the leafy rurality of commuter villages around major metropolitan centres serves this purpose. For others, perhaps motivated by the search for a more peripheral and isolated sense of rural environment, or perhaps restricted in terms of having to seek out less expensive land and housing, or both, the draw is towards areas such as rural mid-Wales.

In his study of the Hampshire village of 'Childerley', Bell (1994) suggests that many people need a big idea which provides both a holistic reasoning for their general existence and a practical relationship with the material and practical contexts of their day-to-day existence. Such an idea, he argues will have compelling moral value, and in Childerley this big idea is 'nature':

> Although the villagers are by no means sure that the village of Childerley is a place of nature, they have no doubt that such places exist. Moreover, they do not doubt that there are country ways of living and people who follow those ways. A close association with nature, they find, is the surest way to identify what those ways and who those people are. The moral foundation of country life . . . rests upon this rock. (p.120)

In our reading of the community studies referenced on p.140 we find very little trace of the big idea of nature acting as the moral foundation of country life in rural Wales. There are two sets of questions to be answered from this observation. First, is the emphasis on nature a phenomenon of the later twentieth century which has arisen in response to the transformation of countrysides into sites of consumption as well production, and to the greater general awareness of environmental issues? Second, has the cultural history of community in rural Wales generated alternative moral foundations of country life such that identity with ways of country living and the people who follow those ways will be more complex in Wales than the big idea which Bell seems to suggest for Hampshire?

What the community studies do suggest is that nature is implicated in, and perhaps subsumed by other major contributions to the moral foundations and cultural identity of Welsh rural life. We mention three such contributions here, although such a list is by no means exhaustive. First, and perhaps most obviously, there is a strong connection between nature, landscape and work, particularly agriculture. For example, Jones's (1960) account of the Cardiganshire market town of Tregaron includes descriptions of 'three types of landscape – valley, hills and mountains – each with its particular kind of farming, but all focusing on this town' (p.84). Even with the decline in the numbers of people employed in agriculture, it seems likely that historic reliance on land-based industry will at least have instilled a realism into the cultural appreciation of nature which will serve to demystify the ideas of idyll and paradise which have been preserved and iconized in the English pastoral tradition. Instead, the cultural record of rural Wales paints a somewhat harder picture, as in R. S. Thomas's poem 'A Peasant':

. . .
Just an ordinary man of the bald Welsh hills,
Who pens a few sheep in a gap of cloud.
Docking mangels, chipping the green skin
From the yellow bones with a half-witted grin
Of satisfaction, or churning the crude earth
To a stiff sea of clods that glint in the wind –
. . .
And then at night see him fixed in his chair
Motionless, except when he leans to gob in the fire.
There is something frightening in the vacancy of his mind.
. . .
Yet this is your prototype, who, season by season
Against siege of rain and the wind's attrition,
Preserves his stock, an impregnable fortress
Not to be stormed even in death's confusion.
Remember him, then, for he, too, is a winner of wars,
Enduring like a tree under the curious stars.

The second connection is between landscape and language. We suggested in chapter 5 that isolated and even impoverished rural lifestyles have been regarded by some commentators as a bastion against external threats to a living indigenous culture. Similarly, the community studies suggest that in some places coastal and mountain-moorland landscapes have provided a safe haven for the survival of key hallmarks of Welsh nationality and cultural separateness. The study of Aberdaron on the Llŷn Peninsula by Hughes (1960) suggests that 'Aberdaron, by virtue of its position alone, possesses optimum conditions for the survival of the language' and that

> In Wales a host of traditional attitudes and customs survives in association with the use of the language, and its distribution is an expression of economic and social, as well as physical, distance. (p.123)

To the realism of nature as workplace we should therefore add the facet of nature as cultural fortress.

Thirdly, there appears to be a strong connection between landscape and specific cultural histories. If Englishness in this respect pays homage to the landed gentry and their country houses and to the histories of industrial and military success, the Welsh rural cultural tradition often focuses on the iconography of religion and linguistic festival. An excellent example of the landscape iconography of religion is provided by Rees's (1950) study of Llanfihangel:

> The countryside in and around Llanfihangel contains many other places of importance in Welsh history. Six miles to the north is Llanrhaeadr where (Bishop) William Morgan completed the first translation of the Bible into Welsh in 1588. A mile from the parish boundary stands Dolobran, the ancestral home of the Lloyd family, and the little seventeenth century chapel which bears witness to their activities as pioneers of Quakerism in Wales. Within the parish is the ruin of the little cottage of Dugwm, birthplace of John Davies who was one of the early Christian missionaries to Tahiti. But more distinguished than any of these places in the eyes of the average Welshman is the farmstead of Dolwar Fach, near Dolanog, the home of Ann Griffiths (1776–1805) who gave Wales some of its finest and best-known hymns. (p.17)

We would suggest, therefore, that nature and landscape have been implicated in the moral foundations and cultural identity which imbue senses of place and belonging in rural Wales. Moreover, it is these cultural traditions of nature which produce particular cultural competences for living in and making use of the countryside. Again, Noragh Jones's (1993) work is instructive here. She characterizes traditional Welsh rural folk as embodying the accepting fatalism of 'peasant survivors' through the ages. Such fatalism includes an incredulity that outsiders actually want to come and make their home in this hard landscape, thinking that it is a beautiful place to live, with superb scenery and achievable proximity to nature. Traditional Welsh rural folk have lived their life amongst this nature without ever characterizing it as beautiful or superb scenery. Whether faced with the middle-class Englishness of migrants seeking a comfortable niche in the rural idyll, or the discomforting greenness of those seeking to get back to the land in non-materialistic and sometimes itinerant ways, notions of belonging and well-being can be disturbed by this clash of cultural references to nature.

Jones, as is her habit, provides an optimistic spin on such clashes. She suggests that the Welsh language offers 'greener ways of seeing the everyday world' (p.179), but even in a (Welsh) monolinguistic arena, it seems likely that the everyday worlds of rural Wales will be imagined differently according to different cultural identities, and experienced differently according to different cultural competences. It is to these cultural competences that we now turn.

Cultural competence and rural lifestyles

Much of the recent work which seeks to understand contemporary rural life has focused on the notion of idyll (see, for example, Bunce, 1993; Mingay, 1989a–c; J. Short, 1991; B. Short, 1992), suggesting that mythological and romanticized constructions of pastoralism and arcadia have invested rural living with signified meanings of happy, healthy and problem-free existence in close-knit communities and close to the natural environment of the countryside.

Such ideas are of practical as well as theoretical importance (Cloke and Milbourne, 1992) since these kinds of cultural constructions can be interconnected with important attitudes, behaviours, practices and decisions: the decision to migrate into or visit the countryside; the expectation that rural life involves a lower level of formal opportunities and facilities than would be acceptable in an urban arena; the assumption that high levels of community support and care exist in the rural; the in-built assumptions about what 'belongs' or is 'welcome' in rural life, especially in terms of gender, ethnicity, sexuality and the like (see Cloke and Little, 1997; Milbourne, 1996), and so on. It would be erroneous simply to 'read off' rural lifestyle experiences from these culturally constructed ideas, but we do want to suggest that different scales of rural idyll, though interconnecting and overlapping, impinge on lifestyle experiences in different ways.

We have already in this chapter encountered a series of cultural identities in rural Wales which differ markedly from these fed by imaginations of English rural idylls (see also Bowie, 1993; Cloke, Goodwin and Milbourne, 1995). These national-level cultural distinctions are further enmeshed by regional-level constructs of rurality, with clear differences to be expected, for example, between Welsh-speaking areas of rural Wales (*Y Fro Gymraeg*) and elsewhere, as well as between north and south, Cardiganshire and everywhere else (Madgwick et al., 1973), and so on. Even very localized differences will contribute to differentialized experiences of belonging, placedness and cultural affinity in rural lifestyles in particular places. It follows from these differentiated cultural constructions of rurality and rural life, that people migrating to particular rural areas may, to varying extents, bring with them specific *imagined geographies* of rural life which will prompt certain expectations about the lifestyle they will live out following their move. Such expectations may well conflict with the entrenched imagined geographies and resultant lifestyle expectations held by long-standing and/or indigenous residents in the place concerned.

We have suggested elsewhere (see Cloke, Goodwin and Milbourne, 1997) that the arena of this conflict will often relate to the *cultural competences* which arise from the translation of idyllized expectations into actions and attitudes. We believe that some of the ways in which in-migrant people do not seem to 'fit' into their new community and place relate to the ways in which they behave culturally – how they interact with local people, how they decorate their homes, how they display various items of consumption and so on. Drawing on the concepts forwarded by Klaus Eder (1993; see also Cloke, Phillips and Thrift, 1995, 1997) the focus on cultural competences suggests that an interdependence of income/qualifications and moral/aesthetic attributes permits the recognition of socially distributed quantities of competences which influence networks of social interaction in developed nations. It follows, then, that social conflict in rural life may well reflect disjunctures between the different cultural competences which inform rural lifestyles.

In the case of rural lifestyles in Wales, we believe that these different cultural competences are a significant factor in understanding the senses of 'well-being' and 'belonging' (or otherwise) that are drawn from rural communities and rural environments. The following comment from one of our interviews is instructive. When asked about the changes taking place locally, the response was

> More English coming in. They don't belong here. They would be all right if they were part of the community, spoke Welsh. But they live as if they were still in England. (2066, Devil's Bridge)

This last phrase – 'they live as if they were still in England' – seems to us a significant indication of the process in which in-migrants from England bring with them a mix of different cultural competences reflecting the imagined geographies of English rural life. As we have pointed out,

When such competences are placed and practised in rural Wales they can often lead to distinct cultural conflicts resulting in an experience of 'not belonging' on the part of in-migrants, and experiences of 'a threat to our way(s) of life' on the part of different existing residents. (Cloke, Milbourne and Thomas, 1997)

Part of 'living as if they were still in England' relates to an obvious inability to speak the Welsh language, which will often exclude in-migrants from 'belonging' to local organizations which conduct their affairs through the medium of Welsh. Nevertheless, the threat to cultural identities of Welshness is wider than this. In chapters 2 and 3, for example, it is evident that many Welsh residents see English migrants as a continuation of long-standing processes of colonialism, dominating housing markets, exploiting the country and taking over rural affairs. It is also evident that localized practices of 'not joining in' also aggravate these cultural differences. Either way, English in-migrants often appear to refer to cultural constructs of the English village when organizing their lifestyle strategies in rural Wales, and as a consequence they bring with them class practices, consumption signals and other shortfalls of competence which are soon detected and made significant by local residents. One of our respondents complained that

a lot of English people have come in . . . changed the way of life. The problem with those people is that they're working on a Sunday – you know, cleaning their cars and mowing the lawns. They shouldn't do it on a Sunday – they should be in chapel. (2162, Devil's Bridge)

Another study-area resident told us:

they (the English) just don't know how to behave. They drive the wrong cars, put up the wrong curtains, and create pretty front gardens that just don't fit in. In the village they don't know how to greet people, how to have a real conversation. Some of them want nothing to do with us, and others would like to be part of the community, but only if they can be in charge of what goes on. They just don't know how to belong, even when they try very hard to fit in. (PC interview with Teifi Valley resident)

We are not arguing here that cultural competence is restricted to these issues of Sabbatarianism, symbolic consumption and social graces. (Indeed, many indigenous people in rural Wales might also wish to contest these constructs.) Neither do we propose a determ-inistic version of cultural conflict. Individuals vary in personality as well as in coping strategy. Situations change, competences can be learnt, and transitional difficulties experienced by, and caused by, in-migrants vary considerably. Nevertheless, we do believe that these issues of cultural competence can contribute significantly to feelings of belonging/not belonging, welcome/not welcome and well-being/unwell-being in rural lifestyles.

Findings from the Rural Lifestyles study

In our surveys we asked respondents to describe what it was like to live where they did. In particular we asked them to talk about some of the cultural images of rurality described above: the countryside as a contribution to health and well-being; the importance of community life; the contribution of the natural environment; and the experience of being away from it all. We wanted to understand the varying experience of what it was like to have a lifestyle amongst all these changes. Why did people move to rural areas? Why did they stay? How did they cope with problems? What did a rural lifestyle mean to them and what was it worth to them? We briefly consider these issues in the following sections.

The Welsh countryside as a healthy place in which to live

One of the questions we asked our respondents was whether they regarded the countryside as a healthier place to live than more urban environments. Table 7.1 records their answers. Overwhelmingly, people expressed a belief that the countryside was a healthier place to live than the towns. Interestingly the Teifi Valley, with the highest recorded incidence of serious health problems, was the location of the second highest level of perception that the countryside was a healthier place to live than towns. There is, we may conclude, little *post hoc* reasoning from the experience of health problems to doubts about the strong persistence of an image or idea that the countryside is healthier. The lowest recorded percentage of respondents finding the country-side healthier was 82 per cent in the Devil's Bridge study area. The reasons given for the healthy nature of the countryside varied, but most frequently included reference to the lack of pollution, or, when expressed in more positive terms, 'the fresh air'.

Table 7.1: Percentage of respondents saying that is is healthier to live in the country

Betws-y-coed	84.9	Northumberland	86.5
Teifi Valley	84.3	Shropshire	86.2
Tanat Valley	82.9	Devon	82.8
Devil's Bridge	82.0	North Yorkshire	82.5
All	83.6		

It's better fresh air. (1005, Betws-y-coed)

Fresh air, no pollution. (2162, Devil's Bridge)

No smog, chemicals from industry, less congested with traffic. (3120, Tanat Valley)

It must be – more fresh air. (4088, Teifi Valley)

The linkage between the fresh air and the more open environment and associated lack of stress occurs frequently. The social nature of rural areas was also perceived as making these areas safer, as well as healthier, although the specific character of the 'urban threat' was rarely defined:

Less hectic pace of life. (1068, Betws-y-coed)

. . . tension higher in towns, stress. (2023, Devil's Bridge)

. . . no rat race, no tension, friendly people. (4006, Teifi Valley)

The symbolism of nature and freshness was occasionally extended to the availability of fresh produce:

Air is cleaner, food is fresher. (2068, Devil's Bridge)

Plenty of fresh air, and plenty of fresh veg available. (2215, Devil's Bridge)

There were, however, several respondents who made negative links between health and rural living, and for varying reasons:

. . . the effects of Chernobyl and the unknown effects of Trawsfynydd. (1222, Betws-y-coed)

... I have more difficulty with my asthma in the countryside. (2093, Devil's Bridge)

... high cases of cancer in the village – lead from mountains in the atmosphere and water. (3188, Tanat Valley)

... these planes ... (4003, Teifi Valley)

It's damp and cold in this part of the country. (4196, Teifi Valley)

In many respects, then, respondents from a wide range of backgrounds and cultural identities did seem to be able to conform with the anticipated idyllic view of rural lifestyles as being healthier and more conducive to well-being than any urban equivalent. A rural habitat was seen by the majority of respondents to be inherently associated with natural 'healthiness'. Nevertheless, it is important to note the minority of responses which recorded discordant experiences of ill-health and environmental problems. In particular, fears of rural pollution did seem to convey a certain perception of unhealthiness in Welsh rural lifestyles, suggesting that, for some at least, the cultural constructions of rural idyll in Wales have been broken down by important concerns over environmental problems which detract from the quality of rural life.

The Welsh countryside as close-knit community

As we have discussed already in this chapter, if long-standing rural residents experience deterioration in what they see as community, or if new residents find that the institutions and practices of the community they move into do not match their expectations, or if the impact of market- or policy-related change is to rob the community of one of its focal points or 'glues' (for example, the village shop or the local school), then rural lifestyle problems and experiences of belonging/well-being will be thoroughly interconnected with ideas of community change. For these reasons we asked our respondents a number of questions about the nature of their rural community.

The concept of community is a nebulous one. The varying responses to the question 'what is meant by the word community?' suggest that it is difficult to define, even though understood in an everyday sense. The idea of community expresses similarity and difference; an idea made concrete by the necessity, or the desire, to express a distinction between one group and others. To relate this broader idea to the information gained from the lifestyles surveys presents an interpretative challenge, but perhaps the 'best' information that the survey gives us is in terms of respondents' expression of their understanding of the community idea, from the prompt of the word itself. These expressions vary quite considerably. Despite such variation, it is possible to discern some sense of a felt (or imagined) relationship between a positive idea (or ideal) of community and well-being. Where community has been perceived as diminished, often the expressions are of regret that something worthwhile has changed, or ceased to exist.

> Numbers in the community have decreased; incomers don't want to integrate so much. (1304, Betws-y-coed)

> Used to be more close-knit. People moving in don't seem so interested in what's happening in the village. (1250, Betws-y-coed)

> Not as friendly; a lot of people moving in. (2116, Devil's Bridge)

> People aren't the same as they used to be. More interested in themselves than others. (4944, Teifi Valley)

> There's no community spirit and individuals are more ignored by neighbours. No one helps each other out any more. (4916, Teifi Valley)

It may be suggested that there were conflicting ideas held about community here, not only within an area, but by individuals. There were generational conflicts suggested where 'young' incomers are being perceived as antagonistic to a more 'traditional' community, and an implied resentment that those individuals with more involved social lives were not contributing to a community spirit. The change in community was frequently understood in terms of social recomposition and rural population shifts. Our surveys certainly did confirm, however, that these broader concerns over the changing nature of rural community are undergirded in Wales by the issues of national cultural identity that we have discussed in this chapter. Clearly, the most dominant experiences of community change expressed by our respondents related to the in-movement of predominantly English people, and a consequent dilution of Welsh language, Welsh culture and Welsh rural community. The following comments are a small indication of this dominant axis of debate over the changing nature of rural community in rural Wales:

There are so few Welsh-speakers left in Betws. I think it has destroyed the nature of the community. (1005, Betws-y-coed)

There are more English-speakers, less Welsh-speakers in the area. (1009, Betws-y-coed)

Influx of people with no ... roots here – only use area for odd times and periods – people who don't join in the spirit of the community. (1205, Betws-y-coed)

More non-Welsh-speakers have moved in. (2210, Devil's Bridge)

We've still got a good community here, but the English coming in don't want to mix ... Also it's not too Welsh-speaking now. (2163, Devil's Bridge)

As more English people and retired people move in, perhaps (they) aren't so active in the community. (2043, Devil's Bridge)

Welsh have moved out, foreigners have moved in. (3207, Tanat Valley)

People moved out, English people moved in and trying to dominate the bloody country. It's wrong, don't need the English. (3222, Tanat Valley)

The foreigners moving in don't have the same community attitude, so the neighbourliness has been diluted. (3200, Tanat Valley)

English immigrants have forced the Welshness ... to change. (3054, Tanat Valley)

English coming in. (4082, Teifi Valley)

Lot of English moving in ... they stay inside. Ones who come in not used to saying hello like the Welsh. Before you knew everybody, now you don't know anyone. (4146, Teifi Valley)

Such feelings were often the basis for a differential sense of community, and many respondents identified a situation where the Welsh population still had a sense of community while the English did not.

Still very strong with the Welsh and anyone ready to mix, but most English keep to themselves. (2066, Devil's Bridge)

Still quite a lot of community among the Welsh-speakers. (2067, Devil's Bridge)

People are as friendly as ever, the Welsh that is. They make the effort, but the people who've moved in don't want to know. (2225, Devil's Bridge)

They are a community. I'm learning Welsh and they accept me. (4136, Teifi Valley)

The word 'community' created a problem of definition for many respondents. Community appeared to be a concept that was difficult to put into words – a taken-for-granted set of social and cultural norms. Many respondents defined 'community' using terms such as 'sharing', 'belonging', 'caring', 'pulling together', 'helping each other', 'living close together' and 'getting along together'. This said, running through many of these definitions were notions of 'Welshness' being embedded within community. Therefore, some respondents felt that the English in-migration had served to strengthen the sense of Welsh community felt in the area, whilst others thought that it had helped to prop up the community more generally, by bringing in money, keeping schools open, restoring housing and revitalizing an aged population structure. Thus, although the change in community was frequently understood in terms of social recomposition and rural population shifts, this was not always viewed negatively.

It is in this context that the information on perceptions of loss of community in table 7.2 should be read. Around half of all respondents across the four study areas reported a loss of community over recent years. A clear differential in perceived community loss existed between the Tanat Valley (36.4 per cent) and the other three areas – Betws-y-coed (56.2 per cent), Devil's Bridge (51.9 per cent) and the Teifi Valley (55.0 per cent), perhaps because the Tanat Valley is less of a centre of Welsh-speaking community than the other study areas. Levels of perceived loss in these latter three areas were amongst the highest recorded across the twelve English study areas, with only Wiltshire (55.7 per cent), Northamptonshire (52.8 per cent) and Warwickshire (52.8 per cent) reporting comparable rates. Such a finding would seem to suggest that the strong and particular identification of community with the Welsh language,

Table 7.2: Percentage of households reporting a perceived loss of community

	Yes	No	Don't know
Betws-y-coed	56.2	29.7	14.2
Teifi Valley	55.0	40.0	8.1
Devil's Bridge	51.9	56.9	6.7
Tanat Valley	36.4	33.5	11.6
All	49.7	40.2	10.1
Devon	46.4	45.2	8.5
North Yorkshire	45.0	47.8	7.2
Shropshire	42.6	44.2	13.2
Northumberland	40.5	52.3	7.2

culture and customs in some areas of rural Wales is responsible for this higher perception of community loss.

Although these issues of community change are sometimes not straightforward, we strongly suggest that they represent a very important factor in the interpretation of other more obvious and 'concrete' changes in rural areas. A sense of community loss can heighten the impact of the withdrawal of a local shop or school, or the building of certain types of new housing. A sense of community gain can accompany specific developments – for example, of affordable housing and voluntary activities such as the organization of country car schemes. However, it is equally clear that the notion of community can represent a constantly shifting negotiation of ideas, kith and kin structures and other social relations. Such shifts were very noticeable in the English Rural Lifestyles surveys (Cloke, Milbourne and Thomas, 1994, 1996), and by contrast there appeared to be a more stable notion of community in rural Wales, not least because community tends to be underpinned by reference to the division between Welshness and Englishness – from both sides of that division. Nevertheless, the notion of community does seem to be tacitly understood as a negotiated concept, and our understanding of these negotiations is in turn heightened by recourse to the broader cultural ideas, assumptions and identities associated with varying imagined assumptions about rural lifestyles.

The Welsh countryside as a natural environment
The other facet of the potential experience of culturally idyllized lifestyles in rural Wales relates to nature and the environment.

Because our surveys were aimed at householders, we have not encompassed some groups of 'alternative lifestylers' whose dwellings may be somewhat more informal, but whose compelling moral values are often focused on environmental issues and a wish to live closer to nature. Nevertheless, some evidence emerged from the surveys to reinforce people's decisions to move to rural areas, and also to indicate that any perceived loss of closeness to the natural environment in one form or another may be a source of discord and problems in rural lifestyles.

Many respondents considered the pleasant aspects of their rural environments as a benefit of living in rural areas, and cultural assumptions about beauty were frequently embedded in descriptions of the area in which they lived.

Beautiful countryside – that's why we moved here. (1068, Betws-y-coed)

Quiet, peaceful, rural, most beautiful place on earth I sometimes think. (2066, Devil's Bridge)

Heavenly . . . woody, mountainous. (3204, Tanat Valley)

Small, friendly, Welsh, beautiful countryside. (4182, Teifi Valley)

In all, around one-fifth of in-mover respondents in each study area stated that the appeal of the immediate environment had played an important part in their decision to relocate to their present place of residence (table 7.3). This level of environmentally led in-migration was much higher than that recorded in the four comparable English areas, with only Shropshire matching the Welsh mean. Again, however, there is a flipside to the idea of environmental attraction which contradicts assumptions about the rural idyll. A range of respondents, from 30.5 per cent in the Teifi Valley areas to 10.2 per cent in Betws-y-coed suggested that significant problems arose from their immediate surroundings (table 7.4). These problems referred largely to the sights, sounds, smells and pollution attributable to other users of the same countryside (farmers, quarries, low-flying aircraft, traffic and so on). So once again we can suggest that a perceived threat to, or loss of, the environmental quality of a locality can clearly influence whether or not particular rural lifestyles are beset by problems. Here there is potential discord between some of the likely needs of rural economic development (the jobs created, for

Table 7.3: Pleasant environment as a reason for moving to the area

Tanat Valley	20.9	Shropshire	20.4
Betws-y-coed	20.8	Devon	17.1
Teifi Valley	20.7	North Yorkshire	16.2
Devil's Bridge	19.4	Northumberland	6.7
All	20.5		

Table 7.4: Households reporting problems associated with surroundings

Teifi Valley	30.5	North Yorkshire	31.5
Devil's Bridge	24.3	Shropshire	20.4
Tanat Valley	18.1	Northumberland	18.5
Betws-y-coed	10.2	Devon	15.9
All	20.7		

example by quarrying, or the upkeep of some agricultural jobs in intensive farming enterprises) and the notion of an environmental idyll which is cherished in many rural lifestyles.

Conclusion: splendid isolation?

We began this chapter with Noragh Jones's account of coming to live in Cwmrheidol, and of the tensions between the beauty of the place and being cut-off by its remoteness, and between the depth of the local community and being potentially cut off or remote from it. Jones also speculated as to how local people might themselves feel cut off from their living Welsh rural culture because the influx of Englishness was thought to be changing the character of the entire village. We have argued more generally that 'well-being' and 'belonging' in rural life are wrapped up with ideas of community and environment. The rich heritage of community studies in rural Wales suggests that a strong symbolic construction of belonging is based on two intertwined axes of Welshness – relating to popular spoken and musical cultures, and to a sense of being Welsh which is defined at least in part by an opposition to Englishness. Equally, environment is implicated in many of the major contributors to the moral foundations and cultural identity of Welsh rural life, including its role as an arena for work, a fortress for linguistic protection and a setting for icons of cultural history. Such constructs of environment again reflect a particular Welshness of landscape.

These cultural traditions appear to feed strongly into contemporary cultural competences for living in and making use of the countryside. In turn, cultural competences associated with Welshness are likely to conflict with the various imaginations about the sociology and geography of rural life drawn from cultural constructions of English rural life, which feed the cultural competences of many in-migrants. Some of the findings of the Rural Lifestyles study demonstrate the contemporary importance of conflicts over community and environment, and reinforce the idea that experiences of well-being and belonging in rural life will be influenced by cultural constructions of centrality and marginality as well as by the more material structuring of opportunities.

The obverse of belonging is sometimes loneliness. Some people will positively choose a remote rural lifestyle so that they can get away from it all to inhabit an 'unspoilt' environment miles from anywhere, whereas other people's experiences of rural living are characterized by an extreme loneliness and sense of isolation. It is frequently the 'isolation' of rural Wales that encourages in-movement. The perceived tranquillity, healthiness and aesthetic benefits of the less populated countryside feed into and feed from an idyll that does not seem to decrease in its pervasiveness, or persuasiveness. However, if in-movement has occurred to an isolated area, the established inhabitants may have noticed (and resented) the migration all the more, because it is all the more noticeable. Again, such processes are intertwined with cultural differences and tensions within areas of rural Wales. Thus, what may at first seem an idyll may have begun to have harmful effects on a lifestyle if social support networks were damaged, or if personal access to the 'outside world' was desired but not possible. Two pairs of comments, drawn from interviews in the Devil's Bridge and Tanat Valley study areas, serve to emphasize that people living next to each other in a rural area can experience the joys and loneliness and isolation in the countryside very differently.

> It's hard . . . when everybody knows your business and is watching you all the time. [A disadvantage of the area is] a lot of people who think they have a right to judge what you do and discuss it endlessly. (2196, Devil's Bridge)

> There's so many strangers in the village now. You can walk up the road and not know anybody. (2215, Devil's Bridge)

Everybody knows each other's business. (3054, Tanat Valley)

... isolation can make you crazy. (3126, Tanat Valley)

The idea and image of isolated rural Wales play a considerable part in rural lifestyles. The constraints on those lifestyles come when an individual or household is unable to transcend the limitations – geographical and cultural – that contribute to this isolation. What is gloriously bleak to one inhabitant is a landscape of boredom to another. What is a generalized rural idyll to one is a precious and specific heritage of cultural identity to another. As in other aspects discussed in this book, we believe that important interconnections exist between the material and the symbolic, and between the economic, social and cultural arenas of rural life. Only a recognition of these interconnections can give a full appreciation of the experience of community and environment in Welsh rural lifestyles.

References

Bell, M. (1994) *Childerley: Nature and Morality in a Country Village*, University of Chicago Press, Chicago.

Bowie, F. (1993) 'Wales from within: conflicting interpretations of Welsh identity', in S. Macdonald (ed.), *Inside European Identities*, Berg, Oxford.

Bunce, M. (1993) *The Countryside Ideal*, Routledge, London.

Butler-Flora, C., Flora, J., Spears, J. and Swanson, L. with M. Lapping, and M. Weinberg (1992) *Rural Communities: Legacy and Change*, Westview, Boulder.

Cloke, P., Goodwin, M. and Milbourne, P. (1995) 'There's so many strangers in the village now: marginalisation and change in 1990s Welsh rural lifestyles', *Contemporary Wales*, 8, 47–74.

Cloke, P., Goodwin, M. and Milbourne, P. (1997) 'Inside looking out; outside looking in: different experiences of cultural competence in rural lifestyles', in P. Boyle, and K. Halfacree (eds.), *Migration into Rural Areas: Theories and Issues*, Wiley, London.

Cloke, P. and Little, J. (eds.) (1997) *Contested Countryside Cultures*, Routledge, London.

Cloke, P. and Milbourne, P. (1992) 'Deprivation and lifestyles in rural Wales', II: 'Rurality and the cultural dimension', *Journal of Rural Studies*, 8, 360–74.

Cloke, P., Milbourne, P. and Thomas, C. (1994) *Lifestyles in Rural England*, Rural Development Commission, London.

Cloke, P., Milbourne, P. and Thomas, C. (1997) 'Living lives in different ways? Deprivation, marginalisation and changing lifestyles in rural England', *Transactions IBG*.

Cloke, P., Phillips, M. and Thrift, N. (1995) 'The new middle classes and the social constructs of rural living', in T. Butler and M. Savage (eds.), *Social Change and the Middle Class*, UCL Press, London.

Cloke, P., Phillips, M. and Thrift, N. (1997) 'Class, colonisation and lifestyle strategies in Gower', in P. Boyle and K. Halfacree (eds.), *Migration into Rural Areas: Theories and Issues*, Wiley, London.

Cohen, A. (ed.) (1982) *Belonging: Identity and Social Organisation in British Rural Cultures*, Manchester University Press, Manchester.

Cohen, A. (1985) *The Symbolic Construction of Community*, Tavistock, London.

Cohen, A. (1987) *Whalsay: Symbol, Segment and Boundary in a Shetland Island Community*, Manchester University Press, Manchester.

Crow, G. and Allen, G. (1994) *Community Life: An Introduction to Local Social Relations*, Harvester Wheatsheaf, London.

Day, G. and Murdoch, J. (1993) 'Locality and community: coming to terms with place', *Sociological Review*, 41, 82–111.

Eder, K. (1993) *The New Politics of Class*, Sage, London.

Emmett, I. (1964) *A North Wales Village: A Social Anthropological Study*, Routledge and Kegan Paul, London.

Frankenberg, R. (1957) *Village on the Border*, Cohen and West, London.

Hughes, T. (1960) 'The social geography of a small region in the Llŷn Peninsula', in E. Davies and A. Rees (eds.), *Welsh Rural Communities*, University of Wales Press, Cardiff.

Jenkins, D. (1960) '"Aber-porth": a study of a coastal village in South Cardiganshire', ibid.

Jones, E. (1960) 'Tregaron: the sociology of a market town in central Cardiganshire', ibid.

Jones, N. (1992) *Living in Rural Wales*, Gomer Press, Llandysul.

Madgwick, P., Griffiths, N. and Walker, V. (1973) *The Politics of Rural Wales: A Study of Cardiganshire*, Hutchinson, London.

Milbourne, P. (ed.) (1996) *Revealing Rural Others*, Cassell, London.

Mingay, G. (ed.) (1989a) *The Rural Idyll*, Routledge, London.

Mingay, G. (ed.) (1989b) *The Unquiet Countryside*, Routledge, London.

Mingay, G. (ed.) (1989c) *The Vanishing Countryman*, Routledge, London.

Owen, T. (1960) 'Chapel and community in Glan-llyn, Merioneth', in E. Davies, and A. Rees (eds.), *Welsh Rural Communities*, University of Wales Press, Cardiff.

Rapport, N. (1993) *Diverse World-Views in an English Village*, Edinburgh University Press, Edinburgh.

Rees, A. (1950) *Life in a Welsh Countryside*, University of Wales Press, Cardiff (2nd edn. 1996)

Roberts, B. (1994) 'Welsh identity in a former mining valley: social images and imagined communities', *Contemporary Wales*, 7, 77–95.

Short, B. (ed.) (1992) *The English Rural Community*, Cambridge University Press, Cambridge.

Short, J. (1991) *Imagined Country: Society, Culture and Environment*, Routledge, London.

Wright, S. (1992) 'Image and analysis: new directions in community studies', in B. Short (ed.), *The English Rural Community*, Cambridge University Press, Cambridge.

8 • The Contested Nature of 'Poverty' and 'Policy' in the Welsh Countryside

Normative and experiential approaches to rural research: the rationale and the reaction

In this book we have sought to describe and interpret some of the major aspects of life and lifestyle in the Welsh countryside. Our research and subsequent analysis of findings have highlighted two main types of information – some factual and numerical, some attitudinal and experiential. This was a deliberate strategy, designed to move away from existing studies of rural deprivation in order to research rural lifestyles more generally. Previous work on rural 'problems' had been overwhelmingly normative in nature, with researchers (or some other external agency) establishing a focus on particular material conditions and opportunities – low income, non-mobility, availability of housing, services, employment and so on – and evaluating the problematic nature of rural life in these terms. Even accepting this approach as the only valid method of encountering the idea of 'problems' for rural people (which we do not) there were several questions to be asked of existing normative evidence of deprivation:

(1) To what extent does the apparent regularity of such indicators (such as McLaughlin's (1985) 25 per cent of households in or on the margins of poverty) reflect the common incidence of common problems amongst certain groups of rural residents in all rural areas?

(2) Do such indicators obscure the importance of localized characteristics?

(3) Do these indicators obscure the different types of people thus indicated as deprived in the different areas (of particular concern here, for example are factors such as gender, age, ethnicity, attachment to locality)?

(4) What difference does living in a rural area make to these normative indicators?

We believe that the material conditions and opportunities to be found in rural areas are entirely appropriate and important concerns for both researchers and policy-makers, yet without answers to some of the questions posed above, policy-making will be a very blunt instrument which will be unable to provide a sensitive response to particular people in particular areas.

Accordingly, we came to the conclusion that normative studies of material conditions and opportunities in rural areas were insufficient as the sole basis for understanding rural problematics. Rather, we considered it essential for variations in material opportunities to be understood in a context which acknowledges that such opportunities are experienced in a variety of different ways by different people. Thus people living in the same place, with access to similar levels of housing, service and employment opportunities, and with similar levels of wealth and income, may experience rural life differently. Their needs may be different; their expectations may be different; their willingness to cope with problems as a part of everyday life may be different; their cultural view of what rural life should be like may be different; their strategies for coping with rural life may be different; and so on. Rural problems are thus experiential as well as material, and seemingly similar material conditions obscure important differences in the way that rural people feel marginalized by a lack of power, choice and opportunity, or in the way that they cope with the strong relative differences in rural life which are accentuated as the affluent live cheek by jowl with the less affluent, with little geographical segregation to mask the differences between them.

This emphasis on the importance of the differential experience of rural problems raised a further series of unanswered questions:

(1) To what extent do people experience the 'same' rural world differently, and are such differences recognized as problems?
(2) Do externally defined indications of 'deprivation' coincide with rural people's own expression of the problems they experience?
(3) If not, are people's own expressions of their problems restricted by different expectations, the fear of stigma, the wish to characterize themselves as self-reliant, or other such factors?

(4) How important are different cultural expectations of rural life as potential sources of conflict in particular rural places?

In order to address both those more familiar normative questions and the equally important experiential questions, we decided that our research should move away from being solely reliant on externally defined 'objective' criteria towards an approach that encompasses the differences of experience to the changing material and cultural conditions of rural life. This necessarily involves an attempt to present a wider understanding of rural lifestyle than just an account of the material conditions affecting supposedly deprived groups. It involves trying to understand how people reflect on the problems they encounter in their own rural lifestyle. It also involves a focus on the juxtaposing of different levels of affluence and cultural expectation in particular places. Only then will changing physical conditions be usefully linked with the experience of difficulties which rural people have with and within their rural worlds, material and symbolic. This approach also opens up new conceptual spaces by replacing an emphasis on deprivation with an emphasis on the wider aspects of marginalization in rural lifestyles. This is not to deny the need to publicize the material aspects of rural problems, or to deny their importance. Rather we are seeking to find ways of conceptually accommodating the material and the experiential, the quantitative and the qualitative, into an interlinked portfolio of concerns.

Such an approach led us into problems, however, especially with the sponsors of the research. It will be clear to many researchers in the policy field that funding agencies are often dismissive of experiential acounts. In their view, for research findings to be policy-relevant they have to be 'hard' (i.e. in the form of numbers) rather than 'soft' (qualitative text which is regarded as 'anecdotal', 'unrepresentative' and 'unhelpful'). In our case, when the draft report was presented, the sponsoring agencies noted that 'Whilst selected verbatim comments are useful, they could be used more sparingly without losing the intended purpose.' The crucial aspect here is obviously to define the intended purpose. As academic researchers our purpose was to produce as comprehensive a report as possible, which for the reasons set out above contained experiential as well as material evidence. The sponsors obviously had other purposes to which we were not privy, and these led them to question the validity of our interpretative strategy – especially that of allowing the respondents to speak for themselves through verbatim comments.

At this stage of the research we began to encounter the difficulties of reconciling the necessary sensitivities to, and competing demands from, the competing sets of academic, lay and policy-making communities. These difficulties were taken a stage further when the research findings became public. We then experienced what happens when the interpretation of one's own research findings is controlled by others – which inevitably makes such reconciliation well-nigh impossible. Initially we presented some outline findings at small research conferences – some academic, some practitioner-orientated. In the meantime the sponsoring agencies had refused to publish the report, and into this vacuum stepped the media. When news of the findings reached the press, they began to publish highly selective accounts. In order to pre-empt this and set the record straight, we issued a press release detailing the key findings. These findings were then seized upon as evidence that all was not well in rural Wales, and this interpretation was compounded by the refusal to publish the report.

The *Western Mail*, the national daily newspaper of Wales, ran a front-page story accusing the Welsh Office of suppressing 'a devastating report spotlighting the extent of poverty in rural Wales' (23 May 1995). According to the report a political row was brewing over the decision not to publish our research findings, and the Shadow Welsh Secretary was quoted as saying that he was 'sure this report is objective and all the Welsh Office is going to do is further its reputation for remoteness and unaccountability'. By this point the contents of the report had moved way beyond our control, and they were being used by different groups for different ends. The *Western Mail* concluded in its lead editorial the same day that the message from the Welsh Office 'to those who are living on the poverty line worrying about their homes, decent jobs and services' was 'Don't worry, it can't be happening.' In the weeks that followed, the story was picked up by all the local newspapers in Wales, especially those whose circulation covered our study areas. It made the national news programmes in Wales on radio and TV, and some months later a documentary film was made by HTV based on the research findings. The refusal to publish the report was even used by the satirical magazine *Private Eye* as a pretext to attack one of the Welsh Office ministers.

The normative and experiential findings were used in different ways by different players in this media game. The television documentary concentrated on the experiential findings, and built the programme around the differential experiences of a group of contrasting people living in one of our study areas. They were thus using the very material that the research sponsors had questioned, and had found it interesting and valid enough to support a current affairs documentary. The newspapers, local authorities and campaigning groups which used the research tended to favour the more quantitative material evidence, as did the sponsoring agencies – but interestingly drew completely different conclusions from it. The former groups uniformly accepted the validity of the findings, although each highlighted different aspects.

In contrast, the sponsoring agencies publicly stated that they were unhappy with the research findings. As part of the media interest, several journalists questioned the Welsh Office about their decision not to publish the report. The replies given to these questions are all the information we have about why the findings of the three-year research project were not published – the sponsoring agencies never informed us why they had taken this decision. In response to the journalists, the Welsh Office apparently questioned the methodology of the research and were also concerned that some of our conclusions went beyond what the findings justified. It seems a little odd to us that they should question the methodology after the event, when they commissioned and sponsored the report on the condition that this very methodology was used. Discussions were held on this point before the project began, and no concerns were raised then at all – indeed this methodology was encouraged in order to enable comparisons to be drawn with the English Lifestyles project. It is also interesting to note that the results of the English research, which used exactly the same methodology, was published in full (Cloke, Milbourne and Thomas, 1994). This leads us to question why the English sponsors – the Rural Development Commission, the Department of the Environment and the Economic and Social Research Council – were happy to publish and the Welsh were not. The only specific concern the Welsh Office raised in response to press enquiries was that the sample size was not large enough to draw conclusions, especially with regard to the specific question on income which we used to construct the poverty index. The sample of 1,000 randomly selected households represents the largest survey of this type ever undertaken in rural Wales, and the vast majority of questions were answered by all respondents. The questionnaire is over 100 pages long, takes up to two and a half hours to complete and contains several hundred individual questions about many aspects of a person's rural lifestyle. It seems a little bizarre to dismiss the whole research on the basis of the response rate to one question – especially as we have other information on income which confirms these findings. The report specifically draws attention to the response rate for one of the questions on income and comments that any findings 'should be set in this context' (Cloke, Goodwin and Milbourne, 1993, 73). Had the Welsh Office published the report, readers would have been able to note this, along with all the other data on income and expenditure, and exercise their own judgements.

Very rarely did anyone check with us before they published or presented their own interpretations of our findings, and in fact, by not publishing the report, the Welsh Office ensured that these different interpretations could develop a currency of their own in the absence of an 'authorized' version. The original academic purpose had been lost, as different groups battled to use sections of the unpublished report to their own advantage. In the middle were the respondents and residents of each study area, whose lifestyles were now public property. As usual, their voices were very little in evidence. What the whole episode reveals is the ways in which the different types of knowledge that we presented were used for purposes way beyond their original intent – with different groups seizing upon different aspects of the research. Very rarely were the two types of findings – the material and the experiential – connected, as we had intended.

What gave the research findings extra piquancy, and undoubtedly added to the public and media concern, was the announcement by the Secretary of State for Wales that he intended to publish a White Paper on the future of rural Wales. In a letter inviting written submissions as part of the preparation for this, it was stated that the Secretary of State intended to 'listen carefully to what businesses, the agricultural sector, local authorities, agencies, community and voluntary groups have to say on any economic, social or environmental issue which they feel should form part of this review' (Welsh Office, Ref.: DB 15/3/280). The consultation process obviously did not extend to academics, even those who had just carried out a major report on the same subject as the proposed White Paper. Since the White Paper has now been published, it seems instructive to examine its contents in the light of the findings reported in this book.

Rural lifestyles and the 1996 White Paper

Given the range and significance of the findings from our Rural Lifestyles study in Wales, and given the varying reactions to these findings from the sponsoring agencies and from the press, it seems highly relevant for us to contextualize the study in terms of the contemporary recognition of problems, and policy responses to those problems, by the Conservative government. In March 1996, the Secretary of State for Wales introduced a White Paper entitled 'A Working Countryside for Wales' (Welsh Office, 1996) which 'sets out the Government's vision for rural Wales' (p.1). The White Paper provides us with an interesting set of comparisons with the Lifestyles study. On the surface, there is an implicit recognition from government that rural communities in Wales are arenas where action is necessary, because contemporary market conditions will not *per se* facilitate provision of housing and services.

> The rural community is not just a place of work. It is also a place of family life and a place of learning. That is why we have taken the initiative to encourage affordable housing, to keep village schools open, to help the village hall, and the village shop. These institutions often provide an invaluable network of connections that bind communities together. We want to support them. We are also committed to improving the services to the people who live and work in rural Wales. In this paper, we have set out new ways of supporting and enhancing public services in rural areas, including health and social services and education. (p.1)

In some ways, it is inevitable that this tone of an up-beat government, taking the initiative, being supportive, committed to improvement, enhancing services, and so on, will be set discursively for the part-rhetorical and part-propaganda purposes commonly served these days by White Papers. The government wants to point the way to a future in rural Wales, clearly demonstrating its own commitment to community, economy and environment. It wants to advertise the view that everything that can be done is being done, and that the prosperity of the future is assured.

Such window-dressing is inevitable, but the questions we want to ask of the White Paper on the basis of the Rural Lifestyles study demand that government discourses of rural prosperity be deconstructed and sifted for two crucial elements of policy. The first element concerns a grounded recognition of some of the problems experienced by people in rural Wales. These problems may be sectoral, relating to jobs, housing, services and transport, but also experiential, relating to issues of marginalization, belonging and well-being. Both strands of the problematic will contribute to a recognition of the issues and problems of poverty and deprivation.

The second element involves grounded responses to these recognized problems. Clearly problem recognition and policy response are closely interlinked, but we would suggest that the intuition prior to the White Paper is that the broad trajectory of governmental action during the 1980s and 1990s has dictated genres of policy at the macro-level, and that these macro-trajectories have shaped the state's willingness to respond, in such a way as to restrict the recognition of problems to those which 'fit' with prevailing ideology. Thus, rural areas need to be recognized as arenas of competition (Cloke, 1992) in view of Conservative ideologies which favour privatized and deregulated market-places. They also have to be seen as arenas of production and consumption, and as state subsidy and regulation of production are withdrawn or reduced, we can expect changes and impacts from a deregulated business environment in which countrysides will increasingly be viewed as commodities. Finally, rural areas will remain arenas of continued regulation and planning as a counterbalance to the potential inefficiencies of market competition in less densely populated areas, and as a recognition of the need to conserve the environmental quality of the countryside as a backcloth to new forms of consumption. In each of these cases, policies for rural areas are being handed down as part of a wider ideological and pragmatic platform of shrinking the state and favouring the private sector. In this way, the last two decades have not been fruitful times for those wishing to promote rational processes of recognizing rural problems and responding to them.

The White Paper peddles its wares under three headings: 'sustainable communities', 'enterprise and employment' and 'protecting the environment'; and here we will make brief comments on the first two of these, which are of most relevance to our research.

Sustainable communities

Both 'sustainability' and 'community' are words which carry with them in-built positive responses but which are often sufficiently multi-faceted to be vague, or indeed devoid of grounded policy-related meaning. Sustainability can pose questions about whose responsibility it is to ensure the continued survival and prosperity of rural life, and may be used to promote ideas about how such life might be sustainable for those who cannot afford to buy and maintain a sustained existence in the countryside. However, the emphasis in the White Paper is on community self-sustainability, and especially on the traditional strengths of rural community which are constructed as being self-sufficiency and voluntary action. Thus, the White Paper suggests:

> The traditional strength of rural communities is a valuable resource which we want to support. There are outstanding examples around Wales of local people coming together to make a considerable impact in developing economic activity, providing local services and improving their environment. (p.9)

The government's policy stance, therefore, appears to be founded on using the resources that are available to support the efforts of local communities. Unsurprisingly, the role of voluntary action is strongly acknowledged in the White Paper, but the exact mechanisms of support for this action are less clear. Indeed, there is a tendency to represent voluntarism as an alternative to the statutory provision of services. The White Paper claims that

> voluntary sector organisations who responded to our consultation exercise argued that they were restricted by regulations of various kinds. (p.27)

Accordingly the expected macro-theme of deregulation can be brought into play, perhaps suggesting future 'competition' between the statutory and voluntary sectors, as when it is promised that

> we will explore the scope for further deregulation of voluntary sector activities. (p.27)

An example of this voluntarist approach to policies of self-sustainability in rural Wales is the praise in the White Paper for the Jigso scheme. Billed as 'a model of the kind of co-operative action that brings together national agencies and local communities' (p.37), Jigso provides low-level resources to help the people in a particular area to undertake a community appraisal and draw up a local map in order to identify what is currently important and to develop a plan for the future. According to the White Paper:

some 250 communities have undertaken appraisals; many have used this as a foundation for practical action to improve the quality of life for local people. (p.37)

There is no indication, however, of whether these very creditable local appraisals are able to avoid the classic problem of being steered by the more articulate and powerful people in the community, whose sense of belonging and well-being in their rural lifestyle sometimes makes it hard for them to see the problems of rural life as they could be seen through the eyes of poor or deprived or marginalized individuals or households (see Scott et al., 1992). Neither is evidence given that Jigso is a realistic partnership between communities and statutory agencies. What resources have been released to help deal with any problems raised by the appraisals? Where are those resources diverted from? Without such evidence it is difficult not to suggest that the strong and in many ways praiseworthy support for local community determination can create a smokescreen for the shrinkage of state provision of opportunities for those rural people in Wales who are insufficiently affluent to buy what they need in increasingly less regulated private-sector market-places.

Where, for example, are the policies for affordable housing in the White Paper? There is certainly recognition that 'local people on low incomes need affordable housing so that they can continue to live and work in the community' (p.13). However, there is (naturally) little or no discussion of the radical reduction in the volume of affordable rented-sector accommodation in rural Wales as a result of transferring local authority housing to the private sector or to housing associations (see chapter 3). As was highlighted in the 1992 Welsh Affairs Committee report on rural housing (House of Commons, 1992/3), the housing associations are now so restricted by the paucity of public funds available to them, that their valuable work is unable to bridge an increasing gulf between need and supply of affordable housing in rural Wales. Centralized housing policies have detrimentally impacted on rural Wales, and the recognition of 'the problem' has had to be tailored to the now reduced feasibility of making a direct policy response.

A similar situation pertains to policies of service provision. Faced with deregulated public transport services which have certainly not improved accessibility in rural Wales – and may in some cases have led to the deterioration of public services – rural people continue to be presented with significant difficulties in gaining access to services (see chapter 5). These difficulties are acknowledged in the White Paper in terms of particular client groups:

> Elderly people and children with physical and sensory disabilities, learn-ing difficulties or mental health problems, their carers and their families, can all face particular problems of isolation and agencies responsible for planning and delivery of services have to take specific account of this. (p.34)

As with the rest of the document, however, there is no recognition here of the rural poor. As our study has shown, low incomes and poverty are very much part of the make-up of many communities in rural Wales, yet poverty understandably has no part in the imagery and discourse of the White Paper. To admit the existence of poverty would be to acknowledge that for many people rural life is not self-sustaining; that community in these terms is in fact being regarded as an individualist concept in which, in the brave new privatized and deregulated world, it is increasingly the individual's responsibility to overcome the isolation of rural life. For all the very positive things that can and need to be said about Welsh rural communities, they cannot be regarded in any way as sustainable unless public policy discourses begin to tackle the individual social needs of people in rural Wales rather than focusing merely on the level of broader spatial responsibilities – which themselves are increasingly difficult for agencies to sustain in this era of the shrinking state.

Enterprise and employment
The tone of the White Paper's deliberations on the economic state of rural Wales is set out very early. We are told:

In recent years, the rural areas of Britain have outperformed the metro-politan areas on most economic indicators. Much of rural Wales has benefited from this trend: its most successful areas have done very well. (p.40)

Against this backcloth, the glaring economic issues facing parts of rural Wales can be played down, and accounts of some of the problems associated with these issues can be put aside as 'common' perception:

A common perception is that rural Wales has problems of low incomes, unemployment, and lack of employment opportunities. However, employ-ment in rural Wales has grown faster than elsewhere in Wales, incomes are close to the Welsh average, or better, and unemployment is generally low ... Not all of rural Wales, though, has shared in this success. The east has done better than the west. There are weaknesses that need tackling. And there are limited areas with more severe problems. (p.40)

Interestingly, the contextualization in terms of rural Britain in the first statement is dropped for the (presumably more favourable) comparisons within Wales in the second statement. Again we can discern here the need to present a positive and up-beat edge to the White Paper's vision for the future. That vision, however, has been dictated by ideological and pragmatic decisions about the role of the state in steering the development of local economies.

A clear illustration of the changing nature of that steer can be found in the work of the Development Board for Rural Wales. The agency was established in the late 1970s, and its early actions involved direct interventions in local economies through construc-tion of advance factories and the distribution of grants and loans to potential job providers (Pettigrew, 1987). Over recent years, however, the DBRW has been swept up in a centralized culture of enterprise rather than development. The White Paper marks yet further transfers of responsibilities away from the board – the rural business grants and social grants will go into the financially capped environment of local authorities; control over social housing will transfer to a housing association; and it is proposed that ownership and management of small factory workshops will be passed on to local authorities or to private-sector consortia. The work of the board is increasingly promotional, advisory and non-interventionist, and its proud heritage as an organization which has made an impact on the lives of people living in rural Wales seems threatened by a slippery slope of change which reduces its powers and budget.

The direct financial intervention which does continue is enmeshed in European policies born outside the privatizing and deregulatory directions from Whitehall. In terms of agriculture, the White Paper is clear in its wish to extend market primacy and competitiveness into the Common Agricultural Policy:

> the Government believes that the CAP needs further radical reform so that European agriculture becomes more competitive within world markets. (p.46)

In other areas, there seems to be a rather more circumspect welcome for European schemes. The Objective 5 status yields resources from the European Agricultural Guidance and Guarantee Fund as well as from the Regional Development and Social Funds (see also chapter 4). The LEADER schemes have yielded nearly £10 million of funding for rural development by eight local action groups. These interventions are welcomed in the White Paper, perhaps because the policy direction is outside the direct control of government, and yet the benefits which accrue can be claimed as part of the portfolio of government-agency activity. Indeed, we might suggest that these European-funded schemes have begun to assume a dominant status in the policies for rural development in Wales.

Outside these Europe-led developments, the deregulatory theme continues. The White Paper promises support for small firms through business services, training and education, and encourages the exploitation of a wide range of opportunities offered by new information technologies. It makes special mention of the need to deregulate local planning through the increased use of simplified planning zones (p.58). What it does not do is to make the link with the specific planned development of job opportunities. Instead, the polished discourse of political enterprise culture links economic futures with the macro-level spin-doctoring of national politics:

> A vibrant and strong economy is the key to a healthy environment, not a barrier to it. In this paper, we have sought to find ways to lift the burden of red tape on farmers and rural business, to re-create that vital spirit of enterprise in many of our rural communities so that local people can build businesses and create jobs. It is enterprise that makes rural life

possible and helps to create that sense of continuity and feeling of community that we all value. (p.1)

The Rural Lifestyles study has shown that there are more important burdens on rural people than those of red tape, and that rural life depends on more than enterprise. The deregulatory and individualist politics of the 1980s and 1990s seem to have widened the gap between those who have and those who have not. The shrinking away from state involvement in welfare and rural development has exacerbated the marginalization experienced by some rural people. To pretend that poverty and low incomes do not exist is to abrogate the responsibilities of government, especially when there are ways of tackling the problems encountered in rural lives. It is to these policy agendas that we finally turn.

Rural lifestyles and rural policies

As we have noted, and as confirmed by the White Paper, Conservative government policies were set within a macro-scale agenda which stresses deregulation, privatization and self-help. This agenda in turn is framed by a discourse which emphasizes voluntarism and community self-sufficiency. The problems highlighted by our research, however – such as the continued need for affordable housing, worthwhile employment and reachable services – do not seem amenable to policy solutions of this kind. There is a pressing, and in some cases desperate, need for policies which bring resources, as well as relatively empty political slogans. Those policies which abrogate state responsibility in favour of privatization and deregulation simply do not work in a rural context where 'competition', in any meaningful sense of the word, is largely absent (see Bell and Cloke, 1989). Currently, and increasingly, those rural policies which provide targeted resources emanate from the European Community, via Agricultural, Regional and Social funds. However, the impact of these funds is spatially very selective (see chapter 4), and with the promised expansion of the EU to encompass eastern Europe, their current availability cannot be assumed to continue for that much longer. They are not the safest base on which to build hopes of rural regeneration, and it remains to be seen how the new Labour government will respond to rural issues at a national level.

The new unitary authorities, on the other hand, were introduced in Wales in 1995 partly with a promise to frame co-ordinated and constructive policies. A major rationale for reducing local government to a single tier was the fact that the new authorities would be 'closer' to their populations, and would be able to identify and meet their needs more 'efficiently'. Despite declining central resources, these authorities still have a duty to provide services and meet needs in a number of crucial policy areas. We have been working in conjunction with the National Local Government Forum Against Poverty in Wales to develop a set of policies which can be put into place relatively quickly by the new unitary authorities. All but two of the new unitary authorities are members of the Forum, and all have been circulated with the following recommendations, as have all Welsh MPs. The recommendations have been endorsed by the Wales Council for Voluntary Action as the basis for public-agency rural anti-poverty work (Thomas, 1996). They all arise directly from the findings of our research, and have been designed to tackle the issues which it raised. Whilst individually they are limited in scope and scale, collectively the recommendations amount to a recognition that poverty and marginalization do exist in rural Wales, and that policies need to be grounded accordingly.

We will discuss them in the order that we have dealt with the issues in the book, beginning with housing. In this area, the following ten recommendations can be put into place relatively quickly and simply:

(1) Local authorities should use Planning Policy Guidance Note 3 (PPG 3) to release land for affordable housing schemes where a demonstrable need exists and where the land can be acquired at sub-development cost. This will be particularly appropriate where the planning authority has an enveloping policy which could otherwise restrict development.

(2) Local authorities should lobby for a special social housing class to be introduced to provide adequate land for affordable housing in rural areas where PPG3 is not effective.

(3) Local authorities should carry out housing-needs surveys within the unitary status area, looking at property condition and housing waiting lists with a particular emphasis on the needs of young couples and young single people.

(4) Local authorities should lobby Tai Cymru and the Welsh Office

for increased affordable housing to rent, both to meet local needs and to compensate for the accumulated shortfall.

(5) Local authorities should develop relationships with housing associations working in their area to be proactive about releasing council land in exchange for nomination rights.

(6) Local authorities should develop policies regarding releasing land to developers, e.g. where a development of more than ten houses is mooted, that 25 per cent of subsequent properties be a low-cost home-ownership scheme or affordable housing for rent.

(7) Local authorities should ensure that their private-sector housing grants policy takes into account property condition and the vulnerability/isolation of the applicant.

(8) Local authorities should look at energy insulation programmes and consider the installation of central heating for vulnerable tenants.

(9) With the large number of properties without mains gas supply, mains drainage and with a septic tank, local authorities should make sure that they lobby the utilities to avoid the differential costs of supplying services being passed directly on to customers in the future, once safeguards on charges are relaxed.

(10) Local authorities should ensure that all dwellings have an indoor toilet.

In terms of employment, the new authorities should put into practice the following twelve recommendations:

(1) All new unitary authorities should set up economic development departments/units, particularly given the changes to the Development Board for Rural Wales.

(2) Local authorities' economic development departments should work closely with the Welsh Development Agency, Land Authority and Wales Tourist Board to attract money and economic development initiatives into the area.

(3) Local authorities need to be aware of European funding available, and may wish to appoint a European officer shared by a number of county boroughs. This is extremely important when we consider that the eight LEADER programme initiatives have brought almost £10 million into rural Wales. European funding in mid-term programmes often requires short deadline responses,

and authorities need to be able to respond to the opportunities.

(4) Local authorities should support community businesses with the help of Community Enterprise Wales.

(5) Local authorities should prioritize community development initiatives, e.g. Credit Union and Local Exchange Trading Systems (LETS), to help empower impoverished communities.

(6) Local authorities should support child-care initiatives to enable women to be retrained.

(7) Local authorities should support the principle of a national minimum wage.

(8) Local authorities should undertake a skills audit of the population of working age to assist in attracting the right jobs for an area.

(9) Local authorities should offer training opportunities and apprenticeships wherever possible.

(10) Local authorities should work with schools in identifying training opportunities in employment as school-leavers have the greatest difficulties in obtaining jobs.

(11) Local authorities should lobby the Welsh Office for a rural development policy initiative that maps deprivation, audits skills and creates permanent, rather than part-time, seasonal and insecure jobs.

(12) In more remote areas, farming is still a crucial employer. Local authorities need to work up policies with the Agricultural Training Board and other relevant organizations to combat the increasing financial difficulties faced by this sector.

In the case of accessibility and services, six recommendations can be made:

(1) Local authorities should survey their populations' transport needs in order better to inform public transport provision.

(2) Local authorities should work through their economic development departments to maintain service provision in villages with a high proportion of elderly people and young people without access to public or private transport. In particular, mobile services are crucial for non-mobile residents, e.g. the library service and mobile food service.

(3) Local authorities should consider grant-aiding supermarkets to offer a weekly 'Shopperbus' service to outlying communities.

(4) Local authorities should consider supporting pre- and post-school initiatives as part of a community development initiative. Support can be given through Chwarae Teg.

(5) Local authorities should consider the direct provision of, or support for, voluntary-sector provision of youth facilities accessible without transport.

(6) Local authorities should have regular meetings with the health authority with regard to local provision to ensure comprehensive community-based transport schemes to ensure that non-mobile groups can access health services.

In terms of low income in the countryside, the following four recommendations can be made for local authority action:

(1) In view of the research findings, local authorities need to be aware of the specific needs of the elderly, e.g. in social-service charging policies and community care.

(2) Since many owner-occupiers are elderly and without mortgages, but also often without substantial savings, local authorities need to be proactive in advertising private-sector housing grants and other initiatives to assist people to stay in their homes.

(3) Local authorities should run and/or support benefit take-up campaigns both for income support, and for disability and work-related benefits.

(4) Local authorities should be proactive in supporting council-tax rebate schemes.

Finally, in terms of living in the countryside, we can make the following four recommendations:

(1) Local authorities need to recognize the absence, for many rural households, of family-support networks in the creation of rural development policies.

(2) Local authorities need to recognize the isolation of rural communities, particularly for people who are not mobile, either for health reasons or income.

(3) Local authorities should consider subsidizing public transport for those on low incomes.

(4) Local authorities should consider reduced rates of entry to leisure provision for low-income users.

Increasing limits on the resources and responsibilities of local authorities mean that these recommendations are of necessity limited. They do, however, offer some reasonably inexpensive and immediate responses to the symptoms of rural poverty and marginalization. They recognize that poverty exists, and they are targeted at those who suffer its consequences. Of course, tackling the causes rather than the symptoms of such poverty and marginalization is another matter altogether, which will need considerable thought and long-term action on national and European scales. The results of our research, which revealed that considerable levels of poverty, low income, marginalization and service deprivation still exist in the Welsh countryside, suggest that the policies favoured by the Conservative governments of the 1980s and 1990s have hardly begun to tackle these causes at all. Recent data, for instance, indicates that wage levels in rural Wales are still shockingly low. The proportion of full-time employees earning less than the Council of Europe's 'decency threshold' (£228.68 per week) is far higher than we might expect across rural Wales. In Gwynedd, for instance, 48.8 per cent of men and 58.4 per cent of women earn less than this threshold. In Dyfed (excluding Llanelli) the numbers below the decency threshold are even higher, at 41.3 per cent of men and 70.1 per cent of women (Edwards, 1996). The prognosis does not look bright when so many of those lucky enough to be in full-time work earn below the accepted European decency level.

A key concern for all those involved in anti-poverty work in rural Wales is that government policy, as set out in the White Paper, seems caught within the twin restrictions imposed by political and financial expediency. The political variety requires the overwhelming tone of the White Paper to be positive, and social and economic problems to be played down as much as possible. It also requires that the legitimate boundary of state activity and public-sector involvement is rolled back even further. Into the space created come notions of self-help and community sustainability – not accompanied, of course, by any meaningful resources or support. This is partly dictated by the financial expediency that requires that the vast bulk of the White Paper proposals are funded either by the reordering of existing budgets, or by the private and voluntary sectors. Unless these twin expediencies are recognized and tackled by the incoming Labour government, it seems certain that the kinds of poverty and marginalization that our research has uncovered will continue to deepen in rural Wales – with increasingly negative consequences for those individuals and families who have neither the income nor the opportunity to participate fully in the economic, social and cultural life of contemporary rural Wales.

References

Bell, P. and Cloke, P. (1989) 'The changing relationship between the private and the public sectors: privatisation in rural Britain', *Journal of Rural Studies*, 5, 1–16.

Cloke, P. (1992) 'The countryside: development, conservation and increasingly marketable commodity', in P. Cloke (ed.), *Policy and Change in Thatcher's Britain*, Pergamon, Oxford.

Cloke, P., Goodwin M. and Milbourne P. (1993) *Lifestyles in Rural Wales,* unpublished report presented to the Welsh Office, Welsh Development Agency and Development Board for Rural Wales.

Cloke, P., Milbourne P. and Thomas C. (1994) *Lifestyles in Rural England*, Rural Development Commission, London.

Edwards, H. (1996) *Wales 1996, Land of Low Pay,* Low Pay Unit, London.

House of Commons (1992/3) Welsh Affairs Committee, Third Report, *Rural Housing 2*, HMSO, London.

McLaughlin, B. (1985) *Deprivation in Rural Areas,* research report to the Department of the Environment.

Pettigrew, P. (1987) 'A bias for action: industrial development in mid Wales', in P. Cloke (ed.), *Rural Planning: Policy into Action*, Harper and Row, London.

Scott, D., Skenton, N. and Healey, B. (1991) *Hidden Deprivation in the Countryside*, a report commissioned by the Peak Park Trust.

Thomas, S. (1996) *Social Exclusion and Poverty in Rural Wales: Recommendations for European Policy post 1999*, Wales Council for Voluntary Action, Caerphilly.

Welsh Office (1996) *A Working Countryside for Wales*, Cm3180, HMSO, London.

Index